So, You Want To Be A PRO?

by
Pellom
McDaniels III

ADDAX
PUBLISHING
GROUP

Lenexa, Kansas

Nelson Elliott
Managing Editor

Greg Echlin and John Lofflin
Editors

Randy Breeden
Art Direction/Design

Cover design by Laura Bolter

Published by Addax Publishing Group, Inc.
Copyright © 1999 Pellom McDaniels III

For information address:
Addax Publishing Group, Inc.
8643 Hauser Drive, Suite 235, Lenexa, KS 66215

ISBN: 1-886110-77-8

Printed in the U.S.A.

Distributed to the trade by Andrews McMeel Publishing
4520 Main Street
Kansas City, MO 64111

1 3 5 7 9 10 8 6 4 2

ATTENTION: SCHOOLS AND BUSINESS
Addax Publishing Group, Inc. books are available at quantity discounts with bulk pur-
chase for education, business, or sales promotional use. For information, please write to:
Special Sales Department, Addax Publishing Group, 8643 Hauser Drive,
Suite 235, Lenexa, KS 66215

Library of Congress Cataloging-in-Publication Data

McDaniels, Pellom.
    So you want to be a "pro"? / by Pellom McDaniels III.
        p. cm.
    Summary: Presents the struggles, failures, and successes of people
of different backgrounds who aspired to be professional athletes and
suggests ways to lay the foundation for a sports career.
    ISBN 1-886110-77-8 (pbk. : alk. paper)
    1. Athletics—Training of Juvenile literature. 2. Physical
education and training Juvenile literature. 3. Sportsmanship
Juvenile literature. 4. Professional sports Juvenile literature.
[1. Athletes. 2. Physical education and training.
3. Sportsmanship. 4. Professional sports.] I. Title.
GV711.5.M373 1999
613.7'1—dc21
                                                        99-26141
                                                           CIP

Dedication

It is my honor to dedicate this book to Negro League baseball players living or dead. Your perseverance, integrity and honor in the face of difficult, and sometimes life-threatening situations, made it possible for today's African-American athletes to compete on a level playing field. Thank you.

It is also dedicated to my wife, Navvab: Thank you for being a best friend, confidante and advisor. You are truly special.

"Continue to Dream"

#77

Others Talk About the Author

"It's interesting when you work with someone for a long period of time, you have the chance to see how they handle both disappointment and success. Pellom has always worked hard and never taken his achievements for granted. He reacts to success and failure in the same way: he works harder and prepares to meet the next challenge."

— **Marcus Allen,** former teammate and 1984 Super Bowl MVP

"When he's around kids, whether they are talking football, writing poetry, or painting, he sparkles. When he stands up in front of corporate executives and community leaders, he speaks eloquently about the power of the arts to save young lives. He thinks about how to make the world a better place for children with the same energy and discipline as he brings to football. Pellom is a treasure."

— **Harriet Mayor Fulbright,** Executive Director,
    President's Committee on the Arts and the Humanities

"He has relentlessly worked to help kids read, to open their minds. He has railed against racism and looked to inspire children with dreams.

"Friday, when other millionaires might be waxing one of their luxury cars, McDaniels was at Crispus Attucks Elementary to dedicate a mural he had commissioned, to give art supplies to children who could never afford them.

" 'Look,' a little boy screamed as he ran up to every stranger he could find. 'I've got markers. Look at that, magic markers.' "

— **Joe Posnanski,** columnist, *The Kansas City Star*

Acknowledgments

I would like to first thank God for all that He has given me. With His guidance and love I have dedicated myself to being the very best that I can be.

To Addax Publishing, thank you for the opportunity to share my thoughts on what I think it takes to be a true professional. You have given athletes a voice and a way to share who we are.

A special thanks to all the individuals, throughout my life, who have helped me when I needed it the most. You may not know what you did for me but I'll never forget.

Table of Contents

Dedication..3

Acknowledgments..5

Introduction 8

Chapter 1 Mile High on Monday Night 14

Chapter 2 My Story..20

Chapter 3 Teammates, coaches, role models 46

Chapter 4 Football: Making progress with attitude,
          discipline, commitment 60

Chapter 5 A dual path strategy.....................................96

Chapter 6 Nutrition, diet and conditioning 104

Chapter 7 You've got the body - now make the grades 122

Chapter 8 Leadership, peer pressure, do's and don'ts................140

Chapter 9 Managing time, managing you 174

Chapter 10 Other success stories 188

Chapter 11 You can do anything.................................200

Chapter 12 Looking back, looking ahead 218

Author bio..222

Introduction

During a time when the pursuit of a career in professional sports is the dream of so many of our young people (predominantly young men, with an increasing amount of young women), it is important to know your chances. The odds against making a career as a professional athlete are around 10,000 to one, according to a 1997 *U.S. News and World Report* article.

To get a clearer idea of how much the odds are stacked against you, imagine this: You're attending a Southeastern Conference basketball game at Mississippi State University. Humphrey Coliseum, or the "The Hump" as it's known in the area, is the largest basketball arena in the state of Mississippi. On this mythical night, "The Hump" is filled to capacity, standing room only, and you've got courtside seats next to the Bulldogs' bench. If you looked around the arena, you would see about 10,000 fans.

If every seat of the 10,000-seat coliseum were filled exclusively with athletes who had dreams of playing professional sports, only one would have a shot of actually becoming a professional athlete. Only one!

The *U.S. News* study showed that 66 percent of African-American males between the ages of 13 and 18 believe they can earn a living playing professional sports. That percentage is more than double any other ethnic group in American society. Often, the pursuit of goals related to money outweighs the desire to graduate from high school, let alone generate the discipline needed to be successful if you reach the "Big Time." Nothing is wrong with earning a lot of money, but, as you'll learn from reading this, earning money is like the age-old question about the chicken-and-the-egg. Which comes first? The money or the diploma? The best route to earning a comfortable living *starts* with the diploma. My life is a prime example.

It is high time someone gives good examples of what it takes to be a success inside and outside any profession. The purpose of this book is to show you, the aspiring young athlete, stories of success and failure from a variety of people with different backgrounds, how they went about pursuing the goal of becoming a professional athlete, and how they handled some of the bumps along the way.

There are the stories of people like Olympic track hero Jackie Joyner-Kersee, WNBA star Lisa Leslie and Kansas City Royals great, and Hall of Famer, George Brett, and me.

When I first sat down to write, I was afraid I wouldn't have enough to share. I was dead wrong. I have numerous experiences to share that have shaped my life as I live it today. Those experiences have enabled me to write with courage and conviction on what I believe are the reasons for sustaining my career of eight seasons as a professional athlete (two seasons in the World League of American Football, as it was called at the time, as well as my National Football League career). These are lessons of life I think all of us can use in our pursuit of what we deem important to us.

So, You Want to be a Pro?

In this book, I will talk about disappointments in my childhood. I was not able to play Pop Warner League because I was overweight for my age group and I was ineligible for a year of high school football because of poor grades. At Oregon State, I blew out my knee as a freshman before being overlooked in the 1990 NFL draft as a senior. These early experiences helped shape one of the biggest decisions of my life: to pursue a career in business and wait for an opportunity in professional athletics.

You can probably name the top professional athletes in America and, beyond that, throughout the world in a particular sport. The exploits of well-known athletes like Michael Jordan, Ken Griffey, Jr., Terrell Davis, Alexi Lalas and many others fill newspapers, television airtime and video games. But what about other professionals? An actor like Bill Cosby. A favorite teacher or coach. The small-business owner. All of these people have the same types of principles and work ethic in their chosen fields of endeavor and have been very successful in their careers.

That's right. CAREERS! It seems like I have worked in almost every field imaginable in order to become a professional athlete. I was a salesman for Procter & Gamble, a long-distance service salesman, a bouncer for a nightclub, a part-time worker for United Parcel Service, a freight thrower for a grocery store chain. Then I became a professional football player. I've accomplished quite a bit to get where I am today. I now have hopes of helping as you look at your career options.

The biggest boundary that keeps you from pursuing your dream is YOU. We have a constant fear of failing in our society to a point that it has become ridiculous. We look to others to see how we should feel and, if we didn't finish in first place, we are judged and bombarded with criticism and opinion. This fear can only be met head-on with confidence and preparation over time. My persistence and vision toward who and what I wanted to be have always been my first priority. God gave me the ability to be an athlete but I set my goals and made all the sacrifices to be able to live my dream.

What is a professional? Is it someone who plays a sport for fun or play? Is it a businessperson who practices law or owns a company? According to the *American Heritage Dictionary*, a professional is defined as follows:

One who is engaged in a learned profession, characterized by or conforming to the technical or ethical standards of a profession; one who exhibits a courteous, conscientious, and generally businesslike manner in the workplace. A professional also participates for gain or livelihood in an activity or field of endeavor that may be a permanent career, such as a soldier, or a temporary career such as a professional athlete.

Because of the commitment needed to become a professional and the time that is spent in preparation for your field of endeavor, professions are engaged in by persons looking to receive a financial return. That return can also be emotionally satisfying and/or give a sense of accomplishment. Everything is not about money!

Hopefully, I will educate wannabe professional athletes on what being an athlete is really about, what it takes to become successful like Michael Jordan, Sammy Sosa or Pellom McDaniels. There is a lot more involved than just putting on a pair of Nikes or shoulder pads. There are a number of steps to be taken and lessons to be learned in order to make the cut. These lessons have separated the good from the bad and the mediocre from the best. These lessons can't be avoided and denied or that dream or desire you have in your heart will never come true.

A professional athletic career lasts only so long, so it is important to have Plan B, C or D ready. Through examples and educational concepts, *SO, YOU WANT TO BE A PRO?* can be a guide that will take you beyond your goal of playing at Madison Square Garden or Arrowhead Stadium or the Georgia Dome. You will learn the basic fundamentals associated with setting your priorities to benefit you in the biggest game of all - LIFE. I have included thoughts on discipline, coping with peer pressure, living a healthy lifestyle, short-term and long-term goal setting, time management and preparing for a second career. The common theme will be setting goals for yourself to become what you desire. After you have reached that goal, shoot for another goal to make the next transition in your life. Develop the habits to be the person you ought to be.

So, You Want To Be A Pro?

An object is first built with our mind's eye.

We teach our hands how to mold what we see.

- Pellom McDaniels III, 1999

Chapter 1
Mile High
on Monday Night

Living the dream

What is a dream? Can you touch it? Taste it? To me, a dream is that feeling you believe will be the ultimate experience worthy of all sacrifice and pain. The first day I ran into Arrowhead Stadium, I knew I was in the place where my dream could happen. I had finally made it where I wanted to be and I was going to take every opportunity to make sure I stayed as long as possible.

Arrowhead Stadium is the home of the Kansas City Chiefs, and on any given Sunday in the fall or winter it is a frenzy of energy and emotion. It is full of fans dressed in Chiefs red from head to toe, faces painted, the band playing and the occasional breathtaking sight of a stealth bomber flying overhead. You can only feel that kind of excitement with a part of you no one else can see. Only a select few have ever had the chance to look into the eyes of someone who is in that place beyond space and time. Even seeing is far from feeling the millions of exploding nerve cells trying to find their way out of your hands, your fingers and toes. The butterflies in your stomach become sparrows trapped in a small cage. The air is filled with the tension of 78,000 fans. There are several hundred people on the sidelines, half of whom are uniformed players, with psyches tuned to fever pitch, eagerly anticipating the first hit. The field of battle awaits. The whole atmosphere really is quite intoxicating, but without drugs, of course. It is getting high on life!

For me, being in a football stadium as a pro - as a player - well, it is everything. I am where I want to be, doing what I want to be doing. It is exhilarating. It is wonderful. It is all-consuming.

Monday Night

In another stadium not so many years ago, just about everything I'd ever wished for in my athletic life came true. It was like a dream.

If it is true that all the world's a stage, then an NFL stadium is a stage for all the world to see each Monday night in the fall and early winter.

It's called *Monday Night Football.* All the players watch it. All hard-core fans watch it. Catch my drift? A whole lot of people watch it! It is a very big deal. And I remember this one particular night very well.

"And the home — of — the — CHIEFS!" Even in Denver, you could hear the roar of the loyal Chiefs fans at the close of the national anthem over the energy of the Denver faithful. Kansas City vs. the Broncos on Monday night, on ABC. Joe Montana, Marcus Allen, Neil Smith, Derrick Thomas and forty-four other guys just as important. There we stood, suited up and ready to play. Ready to pound Denver into the ground. It didn't help that we hadn't won in Denver in several years or that we were on *Monday Night Football.* The pressure was on to perform. We were the only game on television and the world's eyes were on Mile High Stadium.

Even though I was playing behind two Pro Bowl starters, it was still exciting. I knew sooner or later I would have my opportunity to play. As a backup or substitute, you practice the most and play the least. At the time, I was playing so little; I could only imagine what I would do if, and when, I got my first NFL sack. Would I fly like an airplane to the sideline? Would I invent some dance to draw attention to myself and showboat on television? I didn't know. More than likely I would cabbage patch like the rest of the sack masters and walk over to the bench and demand a cup of Gatorade. "Make mine orange, no ice."

Professional football players watch a lot of film. Film on formations, schemes, stances and so on. But nothing on sack dances. I watched as much film as I could of Deacon Jones and Leslie O'Neal and not once did I see them get up and dance around the field. One of the greatest films made was "The NFL's Greatest Hits." This film lit the imagination of every high school, college and professional football player. The images of crushing a quarterback from the blindside or hitting a running back square in the lips as he tries to hit the hole, are still constantly on my mind. This videotape could, and would, fire you up in a heartbeat.

What would I do? When I finally got into the game I didn't have the chance to visualize; I was too excited. It was in the fourth quarter and we were up on Denver and John Elway was about to start one of his famous last-minute drives. He has the most fourth quarter comeback victories of any quarterback in the history of the game. He did it to us the year before and now we were in the fourth quarter on defense and we had to stop him from upsetting our upset-in-progress. I lined up on the line of scrimmage waiting for the ball to move, waiting for Elway to finish his cadence. As he took the ball from under center and dropped back into the pocket, I got off the ball and closed in on him. He scrambled away from me to his right. I continued to run after him. He slowed down to throw. I hit him. I hit him with everything I had. Everything I could control. He fumbled the ball and we recovered. No fourth quarter heroics. No Denver win.

Then I realized that I got a sack. I got a sack on *Monday Night Football*. My first one and it was Elway. I sacked John Elway on *Monday Night Football* in front of the world. What a feeling. What an accomplishment for a guy who was told he couldn't play in the NFL. What an accomplishment for a guy who was once told he was too fat for Pop Warner football. What an accomplishment for a guy who grew up tough and had to fight for every advantage. What an accomplishment for a guy who went to the biggest tryout of his life in a pair of red baseball shoes. My dream had been deferred so many times I nearly lost count, but here I was with certain Hall of Famer John Elway on the ground. Regardless of what else happened during the rest of the season, after the Denver game I had my own highlight to replay over and over in my head.

Once again, the feeling of achievement, of performing well in front of everyone, all my peers, on national television, was overwhelming. It game me pride of accomplishment, of winning, of succeeding in life.

How did this happen?

Do dreams come true? My experience on that Monday night in October, 1994, is proof that they do. Because mine did.

I look back on that now and sometimes I ask myself, "Why me?" or "How me?" How did I get from the streets of east San Jose to the NFL?

Believe me, it wasn't easy. As you will see, there were many twists and turns along the way.

Many people, upon reaching what they feel is the summit of life, will say they wouldn't change a thing that got them there. I'm not sure I'd agree with that...

But, without the hardscrabble life I had as a kid, without learning lessons the hard way (and, often alone), would I have still achieved my lifelong dreams? I don't know.

Someone once said that you can't know what it's like to stand on the highest mountaintop until you've been in the deepest valley. That certainly applies to me.

What I do know now, after being on this earth for some thirty-plus years, is this: I have done pretty well for myself and I think I know what is important in my life.

And I feel very strongly about helping children and young people to get on the right path and stay there.

So, you want to be someone special? You say you have wishes, dreams and goals, that now seem just unreachable?

Well, I lived my dream and in front of 78,000 cheering fans. You don't have to be a professional football player to succeed; the field for success is wide open. Create the next Microsoft. Discover a cure for cancer. Become a teacher. I've succeeded. Others have smelled the roses of victory. You can too!

Chapter 2
My Story

Draft Day 1990

Would I be a member of the Pittsburgh Steelers, Indianapolis Colts or Dallas Cowboys? That's what was going through my head on that spring day in 1990 as I sat alone in my off-campus apartment watching television and waiting to find out in which city I was destined to become a superstar and make my millions. I may not be a superstar yet, but since graduating from Oregon State University in 1990, I have had so many wonderful events and adventures. Now and then, I find myself asking how I got to be what I am today - a professional athlete.

I attended OSU from 1986 to 1990, the best four years of my life. In those four years, I completed a successful college football career, earned a degree in political science and communications and, on the day of the draft, had the opportunity to live my boyhood dream of becoming a professional athlete and securing my future.

I had a chance. I worked out for a few teams, namely the Colts, Cowboys, Oilers and Steelers several times during the winter and spring. Working out consisted of running 40-yard dashes, bench pressing 225 pounds, testing for agility and answering all types of questions. It was great. The only thing I didn't have going for me was the fact that I hadn't played in any college bowl all-star games like the Blue-Gray game, Aloha Bowl or East-West Shrine game. I didn't even get invited to play in the Martin Luther King Day Bowl in my hometown of San Jose, California. That was a disappointment considering I had been All Pacific-10 Conference two consecutive years, and in 1988, led the entire conference in TFLs (Tackles For Loss) and was named Pac-10 Player of the Week a couple of times.

Despite my absence from the post-season games, I was considered an NFL prospect. I had all the T-shirts and ballpoint pens to prove it, gifts from the scouts after they ran you and told you the good job you did. All the memories of wanting to sack Joe Montana and tackle Marcus Allen were closer to reality than I had ever imagined. It was a feeling like no other. Wow! I would be playing on the same fields as Reggie White, Bruce Smith, Leslie O'Neal and Greg Townsend. I imagined my name being announced over the loudspeaker in every stadium of the NFL, "Starting at right defensive end, number 77, Pellom McDaniels." Then the crowd would cheer for me as I ran out on the field through a multitude of cheerleaders and teammates slapping high-fives and, as I like to say, giving much dap.

Suddenly, my thoughts were interrupted. The phone rang. I just looked at it. It rang again and, for a split second, my life flashed before my eyes. I thought, "I get drafted in the first round by the Raiders. I get to wear my hero Lyle Alzado's number 77. I buy a phat (yes phat) Benz, a house with ten bedrooms and, yes, I marry Janet Jackson." The phone rang a third time. My mind was racing, "What do I do? Do I answer it?" With my heart pounding and my hands sweating, I picked up the phone and quietly said, "Hello." For a fraction of a second, I was sure I had heard the commotion of a conference room with 10 or 20 people trying to decide whom to draft and when. As the voice began to speak, I realized who it was.

My mother. She and a couple of my family members called to find out if I had heard from anyone.

"Did they call you yet?" she asked.

"No," I replied, "I probably won't know anything until after the fourth or fifth round."

Then I told her I had to get off the phone because I didn't have call-waiting. Once I finally got off the phone, my heart still beating rapidly, I turned up the volume on the television. The draft had begun.

As Commissioner Paul Tagliabue approached the podium, shuffled the lone note card in his hand and leaned up to the microphone, I imagined my name coming out of his mouth and pictured him saying, "The Indianapolis Colts select Pellom McDaniels as their first pick." I could only wish. What Commissioner Tagliabue actually announced was, "The Indianapolis Colts choose Jeff George as their first pick of the 1990 NFL Draft." As Jeff George started his walk to the podium, I could see his family and friends in the audience. Everyone was proud and happy. What a great feeling to live your boyhood dream of throwing touchdown passes, celebrating with high-fives and signing the autograph you had practiced since fifth grade.

As I sat there watching how much happiness this single event had brought to the George family and the Colts' organization, I thought about my family and where I had come from. Then I wondered about his family life. Did he have a supportive family or was he able to accomplish this on his own? Did he know who his father was and did he care? I found myself reflecting on my life - on how I never knew my own father - and how I accomplished so much without parental guidance.

Then the phone rang. Again I answered. It was my agent.

"Pellom, the Colts want you in the fifth round."

"Okay," I said, "What's next? What do I have to do?"

"Just stay by the phone and we should call you within the next hour or so."

It was about to happen. It was really about to happen.

The first, second and third rounds went so slowly I couldn't stand it. When the fourth round began, I started to get anxious and nervous at the same time. Then something happened. The Colts started trading up. Teams started giving the Colts draft choices. Player A for this and player B for that. A trade here for a player there. Overall, the Colts took five players in the fourth round, and, to my dismay, I wasn't one of them. The Colts didn't draft again until the seventh, and I thought, "Who knows who they'll pick?" No calls from Dallas, no calls from Pittsburgh, Houston, or my agent. By now, I'm sitting on my couch watching the list of names scroll across the screen. No phone calls. Nothing. The end of the sixth round is near and I don't have a clue to what is going on. Another phone call. My agent.

"What happened?" I asked.

"They needed to get some other positions filled, so they traded up."

"What about Pittsburgh or the other teams?"

"They haven't called me, but the Colts are going to pick up a lineman in this round and they might pick you."

I hung up and looked at the television screen as the seventh round opened. I sat back and prepared for the excitement. Two picks to go before the Colts. Cincinnati picked Craig Ogletree, a linebacker from Auburn (eventually, a World League teammate). Cleveland picked Scott Galbraith, a tight end from the University of Southern California. Finally, Indianapolis was up. The announcement: "The Indianapolis Colts pick (long pause) defensive lineman James Singletary in the seventh round." What? They picked who? That was supposed to be me! I was supposed to be their draft choice. I called my agent.

"What happened? I thought they were going to pick me in the seventh."

"They weren't able to make the move they anticipated," he replied. "Hold on. There are five more rounds."

"Five more rounds. First, you said the fifth, then you said the seventh," I said, and hung up the phone.

I was devastated. I sat there and looked at the television screen in disbelief. I kept repeating to myself, "That was supposed to be me! I was supposed to be the Colts' seventh-round draft pick." The phone rang and it was my agent again. "They decided to go with a different guy, but, if you're still available later, they may get you."

I hung up the phone, still unable to swallow what had happened to me. By now Kansas City was up in the seventh round and they picked an offensive lineman by the name of David Szott from Penn State. Little did I know that Szott and I would be Chiefs teammates in the years that followed.

It went on and on. No one called. I thought I was good enough to play. Why wasn't anyone willing to pick me? They all said I was good enough to play. The magazines predicted I would be a fourth or fifth-round pick. What happened? Where were the Cowboys and Steelers? What happened with the Colts?

It was those 10,000 to one odds come back to bite me. Every kid who is just absolutely sure he will make his fortune as a professional athlete should feel what I felt at that moment. Being good isn't enough. Sometimes being very good isn't enough. Don't make a down payment on that phat Benz until you see the contract and sign on the dotted line. Don't stop working for that diploma, ever.

The draft was all but over. I just sat, disbelieving, and watched the names scroll across the screen some more. I saw the names of guys I knew I was better than. Day one of the draft was over. No friends came by to see me. I think everyone felt the same disappointment and disbelief that I did.

Draft day should have been a big celebration. Instead, I came to understand the nature of professional sports. You don't always win.

Day two of the draft arrived and I was still feeling the rejection of the first day. It was around 9 a.m. when my agent called and asked if I was okay. I said, "Yes," but I wasn't. He told me to be patient and I would get drafted by a team soon. I was frustrated and brought myself to the conclusion that if I wasn't drafted by the tenth round, any remaining round was a waste of time. I might as well be a free agent, which was a shot in the dark of making a team. I would probably be better off just taking a "day job." The rest of the draft passed without a call, so I decided to leave and go to a movie. I felt better sitting in a movie theater than torturing myself in front of the television.

As I left my apartment, little did I realize the decision I made not to play football would have immeasurable consequences. My journey had taken an unexpected turn. But, I was prepared, with Plan B in place.

What was Plan B? Because I graduated with a bachelor's degree, I had a chance to interview with several companies before the draft. Companies like Procter & Gamble, State Farm Insurance, Weyerhauser and Kraft Foods came to an annual job fair arranged by OSU. I signed up for interviews with quite a few of them. All my interviews went well, but my interview with Procter & Gamble went exceptionally well, and they offered me a job. I had accepted it with the understanding that, if I went undrafted, I would take a position in Portland as a health and beauty care salesperson. For the position, Procter & Gamble offered to pay my moving expenses to relocate, a company car, a nice expense account and a $30,000 a year salary. Thirty thousand right out of college. I basically had it made either way. I had negotiated a great deal, so I was prepared if I was not drafted and my dream was deferred.

Notice I said "deferred." Dreams are never lost. They can be altered or changed. And they can be deferred. But they are never lost. Only you can give up on a dream, so if you keep fighting, the dream stays alive.

And making a Plan B in case your dreams take a little longer to realize than you planned is always a good idea; getting that degree is the secret. Make it the cornerstone of your plan.

Think of it this way: To become a professional athlete, all the cards are stacked against you. Ten thousand to one are tough odds for anybody, even Michael Jordan. But getting a diploma is completely in your control and your high school or college is full of people whose job it is to help you get it. In professional athletics, it's you against them. In the struggle to get your degree, it's you *and* them. They want to see you get your diploma and if you show them you care, they'll help you find a way to make it happen.

My Journey

The first step in any journey is an event that gets the ball rolling. I was born in San Jose, Calif., February 21, 1968, to Mary Esther and Pellom McDaniels, Jr. I was born to a teenage couple who had in a matter of months gone from the simple responsibilities of being high school juniors to being parents. Being born to teenage parents, I guess, was kind of hard considering they didn't really know a lot about raising a child. They were children themselves.

My mother was an outstanding student. She was able to graduate from high school at 16 years of age. I don't know if my father graduated from high school. He may have received a GED, but I couldn't tell you because I really don't know him. Because my mother had graduated from high school so early, she could go to college part-time and pursue a degree. My father had to work to keep his new family somewhat comfortable, and the fact that he had a child gave him more responsibility than ever. Maybe you can relate to this. If you can't, I'll bet you know people who have had children before they were mature enough to handle it.

My parents needed help at the beginning of their marriage. So, the three of us moved in with my grandparents. My grandparents were a great help to our young family. Mother was able to get parenting tips from her mother and my father was able to find a job, saving up enough money to get our own place. Within a year, we were able to find an apartment, not far from my grandparents' house, maybe half a mile away. But they had another surprise in store. Precious Cherene Denise McDaniels was born on Flag Day in 1970. Now there was an added responsibility for the young couple. I had a baby sister!

I don't have too many memories of where we lived. My mother and father stayed together until I was four or five - then the marriage ended. Not long afterward, my mother, sister and I moved in with my grandparents again. I can't recall how many times I saw my father after that. Or how many times we never received the gifts he promised us on the telephone. I can't remember ever getting a hug and a kiss from him to let me know I was loved. We never received an explanation of why or how they met. I remember riding in the car with my grandmother on several occasions and seeing my father walking down the sidewalk, sometimes in the rain. To think, that was my father?

Living with my grandparents taught Cherene and me quite a bit. How to wash dishes until you got them clean and dry the first time without having to rewash every dish in the house. How to clean a bathroom, empty the garbage and mow the lawn without complaining, to just do it because it needed to be done. I learned how to cook, sew and how to take care of myself before I figured out algebra. I'm still trying to understand how I got through school without my mother or father to help me with my homework after school. My grandparents were there for me and they taught those lessons that are usually saved for moms and dads.

My mother was now somewhat on her own and did the best she could. She worked nights and went to school during the day. She graduated from a junior college with skills as a computer programmer, which she eventually became when hired by Lockheed Martin. I remember Cherene and me playing with boxes of punch cards she would bring home. But those days of working at night and attending school during the day had a price. I found myself being raised more by relatives and close family members than by my mother and father. Soon, just visiting grandmother's house on the weekends turned into weeks and eventually years. Cherene and I became accustomed to being with our grandparents, not knowing they would play an even greater role in our lives. The little green house at the end of Marsh Street became my home when it seemed no one else wanted me.

Over the next couple of years, we bounced around, living in several apartments in San Jose and sometimes with my grandparents because of different circumstances. At times we had trouble paying the rent or my mother was trying to avoid wacko boyfriends while trying to raise two kids. One incident I recall that really disturbed me was when we lived in the Avolony Apartments in San Jose. It involved my mother's boyfriend. I would see him once in a while when he would come by and pick up all of us in his Cadillac, then take us to the park to get ice cream while trying to impress my mother. That was my mother's boyfriend for all intents and purposes, but what we didn't know was how abusive he was.

I remember waking up in the middle of the night to screaming and shouting. My mother would cry and Cherene and I could hear her. Mother would call my uncle. He would come over looking for mom's boyfriend, who had, of course, left. Then I would hear my uncle's voice shout, "Where is he?" Until then, I didn't know what abuse was. I had never seen my mother hit before or seen any results of her being physically abused. I had never been whipped before. That night, I saw my mother with a black eye that was swollen shut and her mouth swollen and red like an apple. From that day forward, I hated my father for subjecting us to that terror though he was long gone. I felt it was his fault all those terrible things were happening to us. We eventually had to move back to my grandparents' house to get our lives straightened out after that incident.

Despite my mother's job with Lockheed Martin, we still lived with my grandparents until we were in a better financial situation. Also, because she had to commute at least two hours a day to Fremont in heavy traffic, she couldn't get us off to school in the mornings or pick us up after school. Both Cherene and I began elementary school living with my grandparents. While in first grade, I was labeled a gifted child, but no one in my family really knew what that meant. Consequently, I went to regular public schools like everyone else. Throughout the week, everyone did their best to be sure that Cherene and I got to school and were picked up.

Not only did my mother work long days during the week, but she worked at night too, so my grandparents' home became my home more and more. While becoming accustomed to living there, I was learning a daily lesson of self-sustenance. With her crazy work hours, my mother didn't realize she was sacrificing her family.

During that time, my mother began dating a man she would eventually marry. She had found a man she thought could make her happy and provide for her and her two children.

If you're reading this and your family life is rough, I just want you to know I've been there. I know how it feels to be afraid. I know how it feels to be confused. I know how it feels to not know where your father is. I know all that. Remember this: with help from others, you will ride out this storm. Your dreams may be the brightest thing in your life right now. Keep them in front of you.

Too Fat to Play

Neither Cherene nor I had a clue my mother was considering remarriage at the time, but just when I was getting used to living at my grandparents' house, my mother and her new boyfriend drove to Reno, Nevada, and – Bang, Zap, Ping! – she had a new husband. Cherene and I had met him on several occasions and he would sometimes buy us clothes or toys as gifts. Sometimes my mother showed up with new jewelry and announced that Robert bought it for her. By my eighth birthday, Robert was my stepfather and we were moving into a home in a recently developed suburb called Blossom Hill.

Blossom Hill was in San Jose near my mother's new job as a computer programmer with IBM. Along with new homes, the neighborhood had a new school and kids my age, so it was exciting to finally have a place that seemed like a family setting. My sister and I had our own rooms; we had our own things. I think it would have been great if not for one problem. Robert was a very harsh man - being nice to other people wasn't one of his things. He set strict rules for all of us to live by, even my mother. Kids were not allowed in the living room at any time, whether or not company was over. I had never encountered someone as mean as Robert. His rigid discipline was something Cherene and I were not accustomed to. It got to the point that we were fearful of him. Fearful of not meeting his exacting standards. Our rooms had to stay spotless. My mother had to have dinner done at a certain time every day. It was a living hell.

Cherene and I started school at Sakamoto Elementary School. It was very nice, highly rated in the San Francisco Bay Area, and educationally state-of-the-art in many ways. That's probably because the kids of IBM employees attended the school. The Blossom Hill area was made up of the very affluent, so Cherene and I really didn't fit in. We didn't know too much about living in the suburbs. It certainly was a different lifestyle. Most kids were into BMX bikes, comic books, trading cards, soccer, baseball and football. One of the best things about it was that parents were involved with their kids' activities and most kids had both of their parents participating with them, encouraging their activities. Both parents in the same household encouraging high self-esteem and achievement were not things I was used to. I think my mother realized my dilemma and, as a bonding type of activity, she sent Robert and me on a father and son adventure: sign-ups for spring football.

It seemed like every kid wanted to play Pop Warner football. To throw a scoring pass or make a great catch for a touchdown, to block the big bully or sack the quarterback. Any kid who ever dreamed of playing football wants to do all those things when he has his chance to play. So my mother set everything up with my stepfather and we drove to the sign-ups at Santa Theresa High School. It was one of the longest drives I ever endured with the man. I don't remember talking the whole time we were in the car. I thanked God when we finally arrived.

While he filled out the paperwork, I was directed to undergo a physical examination. I got on the scale and found out I was too heavy to play in my age group. It was the only team I was eligible for so that meant I couldn't play football that year. I was frustrated, but my stepfather was more embarrassed than anything else. As we drove home, he told me I was fat, I was a mama's boy and other mean things.

When we got home, after telling my mother what happened, he said he would put me on a diet and make me start exercising.

I remember Robert saying, "Starting tonight, 'wall sits' in the kitchen while everyone else eats dinner and push-ups and sit-ups before bed. He is going to lose some weight."

He meant what he said. While my mother cooked dinner, I was ordered to sit with my knees bent and my back against the wall with my arms outstretched. After everyone started eating, I was allowed to join in and have a salad or some sort of vegetable drink. After all of us finished dinner, I had to sit against the wall again until he said I could get up. All because I was a little overweight. Was it my fault I was big boned? Was it my fault my grandmother was a good cook and I was always a willing consumer of her fine cuisine? No. She cooked for us out of love, so how could this guy blame me for being overweight at eight? This boot camp abuse went on for about two months. Then dead-leg sit-ups and push-ups were added. Fifty sit-ups and 25 push-ups before bed. So much for father and son talks and walks.

For a long time, I didn't play on any organized sports team off the school grounds, in part because of my mother's fear of me being injured beyond repair and also because of my stepfather's embarrassment of having an overweight stepson waddling on the football field. Then one incident occurred which physically kept me from participating. A childhood friend of mine named Doug was, I thought, my best friend. We would wrestle, play catch, compete to see who had the best comic books and trading cards and ride our bikes all over the neighborhood. I thought Doug was the first real friend I had ever had. Because of him, I was exposed to a lot of new things.

One day, Doug and I were both riding his bike because mine had a flat tire. I had a ten-speed, but it wasn't as much fun as his BMX bike. We tried to climb this gravel mountain at the end of a cul-de-sac. I don't know why we even attempted it, but we did. All I remember is that we started pretty good, then, all of a sudden, the bike flipped and I was on my back falling down the hill. We tumbled down with the bike hitting both of us on its way down. Besides getting hit with the bike – I got the most serious of the injuries – I somehow managed to cut my knee open exposing my patella tendon and all the things that held it in place. Doug left to get help while I cried like a baby and waited. He never returned.

I was lucky. My savior was a man who lived on the corner. He saw everything and helped me into his house. There, he called my mom with the numbers he deciphered through my sniffling and teary voice. While we waited for my mother, he got out his first aid kit and cleaned up my wound. My mother, who upon seeing my condition became hysterical, rushed me to the hospital. The entire time she was trying to find out what happened. When we finally got to the hospital, I had lost a lot of blood. My mother continued to be frantic and I tried to explain what happened, but couldn't get it all out. I was crying, not necessarily because of the pain, but because I hated going to the doctor. The emergency room didn't make it any better. Finally, a nurse took me into a room and proceeded to open up the wound, exposing my kneecap. I saw everything. The open gash had fat cells around it and what looked like white strings keeping my kneecap in place. There was blood everywhere. My knee was a mess. I was scared, with nurses all around, one with a needle that looked to be a mile long. For me? Oh no! Well, they cleaned and scrubbed my wound, and then patched it up. When they were finished, I had 38 stitches holding my knee in place and a plaster cast to drag around for a month.

Having the cast on my leg was good for something; it meant no wall sits or sit-ups for awhile. When my stepfather would leave for a couple of weekends each month to tour with different music groups, it meant I had a window of opportunity to get loose. I couldn't wait 'til he left town on business, not because I hated the exercise, but because I could sneak into some candy or whatever sweet was available to eat. He always would find out though. How? It's hard to tell. Maybe it was my mother; maybe it was the opened containers of frosting in the cabinet or maybe he actually kept an account of how many pieces of candy there were in the candy dish. No matter, he found out and the punishment he gave me was much worse than any wall sit or push-up.

Until my mother married Robert, I don't think I ever had a spanking or had been physically punished by anyone. Because my mother wanted to have a complete family so bad, with a man in her life and in the lives of her children, she also felt that he should be the disciplinarian. For me, it was a shock the first time I was whipped. I can't remember exactly what I did, but I don't think it was murder. Nor did I rob a bank. Whatever I did, though, it was enough to put this man into a fury. All I remember was him taking off his belt, grabbing me by the back of my shirt and whacking me over and over again while trying to make me scream louder. Believe me, I was trying to hit every note on the way up. That was my first encounter with him and it wasn't my last. I would venture to say he likely experienced a very rough childhood himself. His attempt to discipline me was strong proof.

Eventually, I accepted the consequences of messing up, as did everyone else in the house. It resulted in painful and memorable disciplinary actions by my stepfather. What I didn't know was my mother, now pregnant with her third child, fell under the same critique and disciplinary persecution as Cherene and I. To this day, I still don't know what my mother did to deserve that treatment. She never talked about it. She never explained why she allowed this man to treat her the way he did. This man, who supposedly loved her and her three children, bruised her face and body so badly she had to leave on several occasions for my grandmother's house. Nice guy. Right? The man was out of control and I think the whole world knew. At the very least, the new neighborhood couldn't help but notice when the police came to answer a 911 call every now and then. Was this any way to live?

Moving around...again

My mother separated for a short time from Robert and he lived somewhere across town with a relative of his, but it wouldn't last long enough. He tried to win his way back into her heart by buying her fur coats, jewelry, crystal and other expensive things that only he could afford. He even had the nerve to give me something in an attempt to bribe me into liking him. It was a crystal fish (because I was a Pisces) that stood 15-inches tall. The only conditions were I couldn't touch it, play with it or show it to friends. The crystal was placed in a glass cabinet in the living room, off limits to children. Some gift. Apparently the gifts and some of the finer things in life we experienced came at a price. One day the police arrested my stepfather, which resulted in a six-month jail sentence. When my grandmother found out, she and my Aunt Gloria came and picked up Cherene and me. Little did I know, we were on our way to Texas to stay for the summer.

We stayed at my Aunt Hattie's in Waco. It was nice of her to take us in. It was a boring, uneventful three months. Oh, and hot. We weren't used to that heat.

In August, my grandparents drove down and picked us up. We were going back home to whatever was waiting for us. The drive took two days, just like it took driving down, but this time we drove directly to my mother's home and not to my grandmother's. When we got there, my mother was asleep upstairs with my infant brother. Cherene and I went upstairs, hoping to be greeted with open arms and kisses, but instead were given orders to wash the dishes in the sink and clean up the kitchen. What did we come home to? Whatever it was, it didn't go over well with Cherene or me. Why should it? Cherene cried and I festered at the fact that, although we had been gone all summer, we were cleaning up someone else's mess.

I was eleven and going into sixth grade toward the end of the summer. Cherene and I were not registered for school in Blossom Hill and we didn't have any new school clothes. My mother was distant and we were somewhat confined to the house. It was an unbelievable time in my life. The next thing I remember, we were moving back to my grandparents' house. My mother stayed behind with my stepfather.

Nothing was ever explained to us about the move to my grandmother's house, but we loved it. We soon found ourselves surrounded by other children. Cousins and friends of the family would come and stay for a couple of days, mainly because they had nowhere else to go since their parents were on drugs or in jail. My grandparents were there for everyone. They never turned any of them away. There wasn't anywhere else for us to go, so their home became ours.

At Mama's House

Living with my grandparents was a lot of fun when I was a child. My grandmother always saw to it that we had plenty to do. We always had enough to eat and clothes to wear. She gave us an occasional whipping to straighten us out when we deserved it, but also the hugs when we needed them. Living with my grandparents as a child was a good experience in "old school" child-rearing and work ethics. Things didn't seem all that bad considering we had left an abusive household. I was just a kid; I really didn't know what was going on. I didn't know much about drugs or where they came from, but I was around them and I could see their effect on my family. The effect was bad - BAD! My grandmother took care of us the way grandparents do, by always filling us with love, security and happiness.

The first team sport I ever played was tackle football. We played on the front lawn at my grandmother's house, all the neighborhood kids, my cousins and me. When my aunts, uncles, cousins and neighbors would come by for the weekend barbecue and card party, all the kids would go outside and play football. No fields were located nearby, so we played in the street. Though we weren't allowed to put up any barricades, we did. We waved the drivers to go around because it was our time to play and it was our street. Once started, we designated a lookout to persuade the cars to find another route.

The games usually started as two-hand touch. But, somehow, someone always touched someone else too hard, then the tackling, scratching and crying kind of fell into place. This type of competitive play made boys tough and raised the tolerance level for pain.

So, You Want to be a Pro?

Not only did we play pick-up games in the street, we replayed the games we saw on *Monday Night Football,* overacting the great catches and tackles made by some of our favorite players. Using a car for a would-be tackler, making a spin move around a garbage can or practicing your patented Earl Campbell tearaway by using a stiff arm to battle your way into the end zone was the way we acted out what we had seen on television. Scoring the game-winning touchdown or tying the game up to take it into overtime; we each wanted to be a hero.

Just about every sports fan around my age remembers the catch Lynn Swann made in Super Bowl X, but only a handful of people to this day remember a catch that my cousin Antoine made. I remember it like it was yesterday. I told Antoine in our makeshift huddle, "Go past the truck and shake'em and I'll throw it to you on the other side of the blue car. Okay?"

He went out in a spread formation; I started my cadence.

"Blue five, blue five check it. Brown eleven, brown eleven set hut."

I dropped back (yes, I was a street quarterback) deep to stay away from the seven-alligator (you know the call: one alligator, two alligators, three alligators, etc.) rush of my cousin Lathon. I looked like Terry Bradshaw in Super Bowl X looking for Swann to make his break, then I felt the pressure from a monster rush. I rolled to my right. "Oh, No!" A blitz from my cousin Shawn; I ducked him, then ran to my left. Too fat to play? Ha! The entire time Antoine was working his way into the clear. As I cocked my arm to throw, I saw him get free and begin to run across the street. I had already let the ball go.

Maybe it was luck or maybe it was fate, but whatever it was, it happened. As I released the ball, Antoine got open and started to the ball's destination. He jumped in the air leaving his feet and soaring sideways with his arms outstretched. I thought I saw Swann making a spectacular effort at a poorly thrown pass. He caught the ball! He caught the ball! But without warning, a big crash followed. He had made one of the prettiest catches I ever saw, but he was no Swann when it came to landing. Whenever I think about Swann, I think of someone who was light on his feet, landing like a feather on a pond. Always graceful.

My cousin Antoine had to be about five-feet tall and weighed at least 170 pounds, so there was a lot of inertia and momentum built up. He caught the ball in mid-air running toward a parked car, spread out and landed on the hood. In slow motion, I saw his body go across the hood of my aunt's car like *Starsky and Hutch* (70s TV cops) after a bad guy. It was the coolest thing I had ever seen. He sacrificed his body to make that catch and not even a junk car could stop him. He knew it was there and he still went and got it.

Akron, Ohio

Things continued to change in my young life. Antoine was also my closest friend, so when my Aunt Freda moved back to Ohio, it meant Antoine would be gone until the end of the summer. I asked my grandmother if I could go to Ohio for the summer with my aunt and my favorite cousin and she agreed. So off I went to live with my Aunt Freda in Ohio and I continued to live there when school started in the fall. Cherene stayed behind to live with our grandmother.

At Jennings Junior High in Akron, I knew only a few kids, mainly from our apartment complex. As the school year began, I started to play sports. Because of sports, I became more visible and found it easier to make friends. One of the friends I made was a guy by the name of Demetrious Carter. Demetrious was a talkative kid with an inquisitive expression stuck on his face. His family lived around the corner from Aunt Freda's apartment, in a big house on the main road we used on our way to school every morning. We had some of the same classes together, history and science. That's how we became friends.

Ohio was a great place for me to live and grow up as a kid, though it was only a brief stay. In Akron, I had good and bad experiences. One of the good experiences involved Regina Jefferies, who was in my seventh grade class at Jennings. She probably doesn't remember me now, but I remember her. I had a paper route that went by her house, which was down the street from where I lived. I would stroll by her house every day hoping to get the chance to walk her to school. It never happened. I would hand deliver the newspaper almost every morning. She hardly talked to me. I never really came out and told her I liked her, but I think the entire school found out the day I snapped in one of my classes.

I sat in front of Demetrious in Dr. Duncan's science class and, for some reason, Demetrious gave me a hard time about having a crush on Regina. He kept plugging away until I had had enough. I stood up and grabbed him by his shirt and slammed him on the desk over and over again until the teacher came and broke us up. I can still hear Dr. Duncan's voice as he pulled me off of Demetrious, saying, "Pellom McDaniels, I'm surprised at you. What has gotten into you? Go directly to Ms. Clevenger's office. Now!"

Now I had done it. Here I was defending my honor sitting in the vice-principal's office waiting to get disciplined with a wooden paddle, then suspended for a week because I had a crush on a girl who probably didn't care what was happening to me. And that was just the beginning. Once my aunt found out, she picked me up from school and whipped me, then called my grandmother in California to let her know. Man, had I messed up. After that incident, I had to clean up my act. I couldn't get into any more fights, get any bad grades or I would be sent back to California.

Later that school year, I had my first opportunity to play basketball for our school. I played with guys by the name of Gary Holmes and Larry Moore and I think Demetrious even made the team. That was just what I needed, an opportunity to build my self-esteem and learn how to work with others in a team environment. On top of that, I wasn't too fat to play on the team. Basketball was fun, but I wanted so badly to play football. It took awhile before I had my chance.

You'll find lots of opportunities in life to do the wrong thing. Sometimes your temper will just flare and you won't know why. But you'll also have some opportunities to do right. Did you ever notice how many professional athletes talk about that one decision they made, way back when, to do the right thing and how that decision changed their lives? It happens, and I am living, in-your-face proof. I couldn't mess up again and I knew it.

Sports helped me find myself. The discipline and teamwork were good for me. I was getting into shape, building a better image of myself and getting prepared for success later in life.

Make a quick note: You can too!

Back Home to California

I stayed in Ohio for only a year. Soon after I went back home to San Jose, I guess my mother was either getting bad or they needed me to help take care of Cherene and my baby brother. No one had the money to fly me home, so they bought me a Greyhound bus ticket. I don't remember how long it took to get home. All I know is I traveled from Cleveland to San Jose and stopped at all points in between for what seemed like a week. I still don't know how I made it home.

When I got to Chicago, I struggled with the decision to continue to San Jose or just get off the bus and disappear. I was too scared of what would happen to me, what kind of punishment I would receive once they found out I had run away. The more I thought about the situation in San Jose, the closer I came to just walking away from the bus station. Even at my young age, I displayed some good judgment. I stayed on the bus and continued my westward journey. Who wants to be homeless at twelve?

Once I arrived in San Jose, Cherene and I were happy to see each other, but I realized our childhood was slowly being taken from us.

We didn't really know each other and were trying to patch together what was left of our brother-sister relationship.

When we finally got to my grandmother's house, she announced to my mother, "Look who's here! It's your son - Boobie (my nickname)." But my mother couldn't keep her eyes open long enough to see who I was or even acknowledge that I was in the room. All I saw was a woman who looked like my mother asleep in the living room. I didn't feel like I missed this woman I was looking at. I didn't know her and I didn't think she cared about me. So why should I care about her? I didn't know it at the time, but it was one of the most difficult moments of my life.

By now, my grandmother had not only my mother living with her, but also her daughter's three children and one of her sons living part-time with her. We had a full house and I hated being there. I hated going to bed at night because I didn't know what the night would bring. Sometimes my mother went out at night. When she did, she often didn't come home for days at a time, which would worry my grandparents. Cherene and I just shut it all out. I didn't care. As far as I was concerned, my mother didn't exist. I couldn't afford to worry about a person who didn't allow her children to have a household or a normal life. I was going up and down like an emotional roller coaster. One minute, things seemed better than they were, then the bottom fell out. When the phone rang at night, I wondered where she was calling from or if someone was calling to tell us she was dead. I didn't know what to think or what to do. I became numb and distant from everyone. All I wanted to do was get away or go away. As in go away to college - but I knew that would have to wait a while.

Chapter 3
Teammates, coaches, role models

Silver Creek High School

In San Jose, I attended Fisher Junior High for a year. During that time, I began to hear some of the terrible things that went on at the high school in the area. And guess what – I decided I didn't want to go to school in my neighborhood. I had to find a way to another. I told my grandmother about my decision and she wondered why. Overfelt High School was the same high school my mother and all of her brothers and sisters attended. It was the same school my father and his sister attended. What was the problem?

I told her about some of the things going on at the school, gangs, drugs and all of the fighting. Yes, I had friends from grade school who went to Overfelt, but I didn't want to attend because I knew that school wouldn't give me the best shot to be successful. I knew the best place for me to go to high school was somewhere away from all of that. A place where I could have a chance.

Somehow, I convinced my grandmother to take me to Yerba Buena High School to see if there was any chance of going there in the fall, but I was turned away. The main reason: I was outside the school's geographical area and the school district was structured to support only the kids who lived in that area. Then we tried the newest high school - a magnet school, Independence High School. It was the biggest high school ever built in the Bay Area. It had everything: a stadium for football, two practice fields, two baseball fields, two softball fields, two basketball gyms, a wrestling room and more that I never had a chance to see. If I could have gotten into Independence, it would have been awesome. The administrators said they already accepted all the applications they could for the school year, but would put me on a waiting list. I was running out of options fast.

My grandmother came up with another idea. I could live at my great-grandmother's house and attend Del Marr High School, which was a pretty good high school. But no kids my age lived in that neighborhood. I also didn't know the area as well as I knew East San Jose. My options were basically down to two schools, Overfelt and Del Marr, with the slim possibility of getting into Independence High School. Time was running out because summer was almost over. Well, as God opened all eyes to see, it just so happened my uncle and aunt moved into a new neighborhood that had a spanking new high school. I had never heard of the school, but because it was new, I was pretty sure it was the right place for me. After talking it over with my grandparents, my Uncle Benny and my Aunt Doris let me use their address so that I could attend Silver Creek High School - while still living with my grandparents.

I'll say right now I went there with a clear conscience though I didn't live at Uncle Benny's and Aunt Doris' house. Considering the reasons that caused me to look for a school to attend outside my school district, I had no guilty feeling whatsoever about using my relative's address. It was a totally different situation than a person who jumps to another school district solely to play for a particular coach or on a particular athletic team. As I said, I needed a chance to steer my life in the right direction. My best chance to do that was at Silver Creek High.

That week, my grandmother and I went over to the school, and picked up the applications, talked to the academic advisors about classes for the fall and took a tour. We filled out all the paperwork and submitted it to the school as instructed. Within two weeks, I was accepted without a problem. Getting into the school was the easy part. The biggest challenge was the bus ride. From my grandmother's house to Silver Creek was at least ten miles, 15 minutes by car and a trek by city bus that took me at least 30 to 45 minutes depending on traffic. Before the end of the summer, I had my routine down. I awoke at 5 a.m. with my grandfather and got to the bus stop by 5:45 a.m. to catch bus number 25. That bus took me from the corner of Story and King to Eastridge Mall where I transferred to bus number 70 that went to Evergreen College. I got off at a stop along the route that was close to the school and walked the rest of the way to campus. At the end of the summer, I anticipated the opportunity to begin a new chapter in my life on my own.

So began my four-year journey, which I initiated and now recognize as the single most important decision leading to my success. The first day at Silver Creek was nerve-racking and kind of scary simply because I didn't know anyone in any of my classes. They didn't seem ready to accept anyone outside the crowd, except one student named Eric Luescher. Eric and I first met in Mr. Mark

Okudas' Intro to Science class and became pretty good friends part-ly because we both played football on the freshman-sophomore football team. After I met Eric, he introduced me to Mike Cox and the three of us soon became best friends. In fact, Eric was one of those responsible for me trying out for football my freshman year.

The other person who encouraged me to try out for football became one of the major, if not the biggest, influence in my life. He was the first man ever to have an impact on how I felt about myself. He was also the first to teach me how important goal-set-ting was to my future and the real importance of an education. He was the head varsity football coach, Alvin Haymond. Coach Haymond was a brash looking man in his mid-to-late forties with a deep, James Earl Jones voice.

I later found out something very interesting about him. He had played in the NFL. He had already been where I wanted to go. He knew what it took to play in the NFL and I wanted to learn. Before the Baltimore Colts drafted him in 1964 as a running back, Coach Haymond was a standout scholar-athlete at Southern University. He understood the importance of discipline in all that you do. For nine years in the NFL, Haymond played running back, but also had a knack for returning punts and kickoffs. I also looked up to him and respected him because he was an African-American man who cared about me and affirmed the potential he saw in me.

The first day I met him, I was walking to PE class and he stopped me. It was probably my most memorable day in high school.

"Young man, excuse me. Young man, are you a freshman?"

"Yes," I replied.

"Do you want to play football?"

"Yes," I again replied.

"Meet me tomorrow morning at six in the weight room. Okay?"

I said I would and never turned back.

That former professional athlete could still bench press more than 300 pounds and squat even more. He ran with the teenagers and laughed along the way. That was where I got the chance to use and develop my work ethic and determination to get up and go for what I wanted. Coach Haymond became the major male figure in my life. Because of him I learned a lot of lessons that have become part of me. I continue to pass them on to other kids.

The next day, after school, I showed up in the gym where I asked the coaches, "How do I sign up for the football team?" Coach Haymond was there with Mr. Okuda, my science teacher, and Mr. Slayton, my algebra teacher. They did not know the impact they would have on my life. They gave me all the paperwork I needed to play, then told me to take the papers home to be signed by my grandmother and have my doctor fill out the rest. I thought to myself, "That's all and I can play football. I'll have it done by tomorrow."

As I rode home on the bus, all I could think about was playing high school football. I had a chance to play for the Silver Creek Raiders.

I got home around 5 p.m. and told my grandmother what happened. I asked if she could fill out the paperwork so I could play and make a doctor's appointment for me to undergo a physical. I don't recall how long it actually took, but I do know I was eligible to play by the third game of the season. When I handed all the completed paperwork to Coach Haymond, he asked if there was a number I wanted to wear.

I answered with a smile, "Number 77."

He took me down to the freshman locker room and showed me my locker and combination lock. Man, was I happy. The happiest I had been in a long time.

When I started playing, it sank in. I was finally playing the sport I dreamed about since I was eight years old. I was on the high school football team!

I thought, "Now I can do almost anything."

I wore my jersey around campus on Fridays like all the other guys on the team, but wearing mine made me feel ten feet tall. It gave me confidence and it felt great to be known as a football player. My freshman team wasn't very good though. We had some good players, but just didn't seem to work as a team all the time.

We played eight games that season and, unfortunately, I don't remember anyone in my family coming to see me play. I don't even remember anyone in my family asking how I did, or if I needed a ride after the game. If I missed the city bus, Coach Haymond or Eric's or Mike's parents gave me a ride home. I realized more than anything, I guess, I played football for myself.

My highlight as a freshman came in the last game of the season. Probably the biggest dream for anyone who has ever played football is scoring a touchdown and I got mine. We were playing Independence High School in their stadium and losing badly. Andre Riley ran for 230 yards and we were on the verge of being shut out. We were playing defense most of the game. Their quarterback, Steve Kemp, who later played at the University of Oregon, dropped back to hand the ball off. I just ran through, took the ball out of his hands and ran toward the goal line. I remember jumping up and down in the end zone, not necessarily because I scored, but because we didn't allow them to blow us out and embarrass us. If we kept on fighting and playing, I thought, something good would happen. I just happened to be the one to make the play. It felt good.

Because I was one of the bigger kids on the freshman football team and showed some talent, the coaches decided to bring a couple of us up to varsity for the last game. If I recall correctly, it was Eric Luescher, Mike Cox and me who were allowed to practice with the varsity team that week. It was good and bad. Because I was probably the biggest kid on the freshman football team and one of the biggest in my class, the juniors and seniors on the varsity team picked on me. I think Coach Haymond brought us up to varsity because he thought it would be a good time for us to get mentally and physically tough. It was kind of like an initiation before the next season. After warm-ups, the coach called us all up for a drill that some loved and some hated: "Bull in the Ring." I don't know when my turn came, but all I know is I was in the middle of the ring and was I intimidated by the chatter.

Some of the varsity members said, "We're coming to get you, McDaniels!" Or they screamed, "Watch out behind you,

McDaniels!" Then someone yelled out a number and I remember getting hit as I turned to find out where it was coming from. Bam! Flat on my back. Never saw him coming. Hit by one of the largest and meanest people I ever encountered in high school. I don't remember his name, but he kicked my butt again later in the year when I went out for the wrestling team. It made me tough, but it hurt at the time.

After that first football season, it was obvious I wanted to continue to play. I had found something I was good at and enjoyed. Football took my mind off the other things going on in my life. Plus, I learned the week before the last varsity game I had a future with the varsity team, which meant I gained a little more respect on campus. If you want something, you make your opportunities, you don't wait for them. Because of football, I created an opportunity to raise my self-esteem and my self-worth. At that time, it would have been my own fault if I couldn't play. Although he never knew it, Coach Haymond became my inspiration, my role model. He helped give me the tools to succeed.

He wasn't the only one. Others contributed to my growth from a young man to a man both in and outside the classroom. When Coach Haymond stepped down as the varsity head coach, Jeff Borges replaced him. A lean man, he was an avid triathlete, so we thought we had the wrong coach when it came to conditioning, but he wasn't bad. In fact, he was actually great. Without his help, I don't think I would have had the chance to get a scholarship to college.

From those coaches, and others, I learned many lessons. I learned how to set my priorities to achieve short-term and long-term goals, discipline in study and practice habits that would carry over into real life, and how to make the choice to pursue attainable dreams through hard work and preparation.

My old track coach Bob Pointer tells this story to young athletes about this kid who would stay after practice for two hours throwing the discus. He says:

"We had this kid here once who would stay after school every day practicing the discus. It never failed. Every day after practice, he would throw an extra 50 to 100 times to make himself that much better. From one track season to the next, for four years, without a doubt. With every meet, he would get better and better. He may not have thrown the discus or the shot any farther than he did the day before, but his technique got better and better.

"By the time his senior year came, he set the school record in the discus throw and shot put and won the league and regional finals several times. From concentrating and practicing so hard on his technique, he could now control his destiny in his events. During the finals in the discus competition, in the regional section that qualifies you for the state meet, he fell out of the ring twice and only had one throw left to make the cut. With one throw to go, he smiled and told himself, 'Just do it, you know how, you've done it before.' And he did. Not only did he qualify for the state championships, he also set a new personal record and won the competition to qualify for the state meet."

I love to hear Mr. Pointer tell that story because it's about me. I worked very hard in high school to achieve success beyond the football field or the track. Those extra hours after practice taught me that a little extra effort never hurt. In fact, the additional time paid off in the long run.

That attitude also paid off for me in school. I may have been a better than average high school athlete, but I was an average student. In some classes I had to work harder at studying to get the grades I did. In the beginning, physical education and art were my best subjects, but I knew I had to work harder at getting better grades in school. I had to increase my grade point average to qualify for a scholarship by improving my grades in math, science and English.

That's where the big three - attitude, discipline and commitment - become important. I dedicated myself to the extra work it took to improve in those subjects, even though they were difficult for me. Just like my extra 100 throws a day in discus, extra work in math paid off in better grades.

Let me leave you with one big hint from this chapter. If you read carefully you noticed that I was becoming a very organized person. I plotted out my bus route well before the first day; I did not want to be late. I carried that same attitude into my studies, writing down assignments and taking notes. Being organized in the classroom is like preparing for the game of the week in football. It gives you the winning edge.

Being a role model

What exactly is a role model? Is it someone who helps young adults pattern their lives? Is it someone who inspires them to think about what they want to be, what they want to do and how they'll contribute to communities? Do role models represent all walks of life and help others realize their possibilities? What do you think?

Be honest. You've been thinking your role model is the one with the smoothest moves. Right? On the basketball court, on the ice or wherever, your role model is the one who's dazzled you. That's okay, but look beyond that.

Although Lisa Leslie followed Cheryl Miller at USC, she didn't idolize Miller. In fact, she knew little about Miller during her stellar career with the Women of Troy. Leslie's idol played for the Los Angeles Lakers at the time, James Worthy.

"I never saw Cheryl Miller play even though we were in the same town," Leslie says. "I idolized James Worthy because he was a go-to player. He was a man the Lakers always relied on and I made the goal that one day I wanted to be a person my team relied on for scoring."

Roy Williams, the head basketball coach at the University of Kansas, was an assistant coach under Dean Smith at North Carolina when James Worthy played there. Williams has often said Worthy's nickname with the Tar Heels was "Big Game" James.

Did you know that Worthy is now a successful businessman? He has taken his big game beyond the basketball court. And Cheryl Miller? Lisa Leslie knows a lot more about her these days because

Miller is a coach in the WNBA. Miller has also served as a basketball commentator during telecasts.

A good role model can provide a window for you to see the future and how to live life to the fullest right now. The role model must have ethical and professional behavior that leaves a long, strong positive impression on those watching. A role model must have a positive attitude toward work. A role model must take the time to raise other topics that are uncomfortable. What does it feel like to do what you do? A role model must be able to talk about the challenge of a dual career, balancing professional and personal aspects of life.

Role models are people whose actions and lives provide inspiration. If they are good role models, we want to aim our lives so that we can grow up like them. While growing up, I had several. First and foremost, I looked up to my great-grandmother, Rosa Clay, then to my high school football coach, Alvin Haymond. Among the professional athletes, I looked up to Lynn Swann of the Pittsburgh Steelers and Julius "Dr. J" Erving of the Sixers. We need role models to show what's possible for us. Too often lately, public figures we look up to, including politicians, athletes and movie stars, behave in less than desirable ways. Too often, adults we look up to are obsessed with wealth and personal gain.

Consider this. Each time you venture out in public, you are being watched by someone else who, in turn, becomes someone else's role model, and so on. If you need a role model, just look around. Pro Football Hall of Fame receiver Steve Largent was elected to the U.S. House of Representatives. Baseball Hall of Fame pitcher Jim Bunning is a U.S. Senator. J.C. Watts, who never played in the

NFL but distinguished himself in college football with the Oklahoma Sooners, is also a high-ranking member of Congress. People forget that Bill Cosby was a track athlete at Temple University and singer Garth Brooks threw the javelin at Oklahoma State. Former Knicks star and ex-Senator Bill Bradley is testing the waters for a run at the presidency.

So what is a role model? You are a role model! It doesn't take long for you to be thrust into the spotlight. If you end up playing a revenue-producing sport at a major college, you will quickly find out what it's like to be a role model. The first time you step out of the locker room as a freshman in a post-game situation, you'll see kids and admirers waiting for you. Don't be surprised if they ask for your autograph.

Even if you aren't a star athlete, or an athlete at all, you are probably a role model for somebody and don't even know it.

Basketball star Rebecca Lobo and her University of Connecticut teammates encountered a unique situation during their national championship season in 1994-95. The excitement of the school's success in the men's and women's programs that year made the players celebrities throughout the state and sometimes in the most odd places. Like church.

"At one point during the mass, the priest wanted to recognize that we were in attendance," said Lobo. "Everyone in the church gave us a standing ovation. We were in the House of God and when that happens it makes you feel pretty special."

Jocks and entertainers are admired by children and adults alike. Why? When you're a fan, you admire certain things about the distinct personalities of the athletes you follow. It may be the little things like how they wear their mustache or hat, what color shoes they wear or the way they run. When fans see them on television, in magazines or at a public appearance, they will admire them. How many kids wear baggy pants or Air Jordan sneakers? Hundreds of thousands of kids have been influenced by rap artists, basketball players and other highly visible people.

If you buck the 10,000 to one odds and become one of them, will you be prepared to be a good role model? You don't have to wait to find out.

Start practicing that part of your game now - and make it part of your daily routine.

Check yourself
Be the hero that others need.

Chapter 4

Football: Making progress with attitude, discipline, commitment

Football Camp

The summer before my senior year, I saved up as much money as I could to attend my first college football camp at the University of California-Berkeley. Not only was I on a college campus learning some fundamentals of the sport I loved, I also saw what a four-year college campus was like. Something I had never been exposed to. It was great. And, hopefully, my football skills would get me to a big school like Cal.

My Aunt Maudie and Uncle Wilburt lived in Oakland, which was close to the university, so they picked me up from San Jose and helped me check in at the camp dormitory. The camp was great. We got up at 6 a.m., ate breakfast, then got ready for practice just like in college. The first few days were not easy, but after the initial shock, I was able to show my stuff and impress the coaches. I ran bag drills, rope drills, pass rushed in one-on-one drills and displayed my knowledge of the game of football. Camp lasted five days and football wasn't all that I experienced during my brief stay.

When we had our free time, I walked around campus, and, while looking at the different buildings, daydreamed of one day walking to class with a backpack over my shoulder. Attending college became an even bigger goal for me and I was close to achieving it. That was the best experience I had ever had to that point in my life. Not only was I offered a college scholarship to Cal-Berkeley, I paid for camp myself. Yes, I paid for it. It was something *I* earned. Because *I* wanted it so badly.

Getting prepared to succeed

When we started summer practices in high school, I was ready to go. I worked all summer to get better and stronger. I wanted to be prepared for a great senior year. I didn't accept a scholarship offer to Cal-Berkeley because I wanted to wait until after my senior season. By the time it started, I had received letters from Oklahoma, the University of Oregon, UCLA and others. What an exciting time it was for me! All the possibilities of my future, all the opportunities to live my dream of going to college and playing professional football were so close. But fate wasn't entirely in my corner yet. My team finished 0-9-1. We worked so hard as a team all summer and practiced so diligently during the school year, it was disappointing not to win a single game. The tie was our homecoming game, which ended 3-3. Although I played well and the letters kept coming in, they weren't the same. The larger schools didn't seem to be as interested as they once were. Smaller schools began to send letters. The Division I-A schools that stuck by me were Texas-El Paso, Washington State, Oregon State and San Jose State. I had two months to decide. But when I was ready, would they still be there?

When the recruiting process began, a lot of stuff was going on behind the scenes I didn't know about. Nor did my grandparents or anyone in my family. We got phone calls and letters, but that was all we were exposed to. As a college recruit, you are allowed four official trips to visit the campus of the school recruiting you. I took all four of mine. When I went to UTEP, they put my name in lights on the jumbo screen and fed me barbecue until I couldn't walk. The recruiters also bragged about their School of Architecture, since they knew of my interest in the subject. It was a good one. A simple trip down the street to San Jose State made for a nice conversation and a couple of future friends, David Diaz-Infante, Denver Broncos, and James Saxon, Kansas City Chiefs, in the NFL. Then it came down to the last two – Oregon State and Washington State.

Both were rebuilding, so they needed good players to play as freshmen, which sounded like a great opportunity. I visited Washington State first. The trip was in late December and the weather was brisk in the state of Washington. It was a nice trip and I really enjoyed the campus. That is, until I went to Oregon State.

When I flew into Oregon, all I could do was marvel at the trees and the smell of fresh air. I was instantly in love with the place. This was where I wanted to get my degree. I was disappointed Cal didn't continue to recruit me as heavily as I anticipated after my senior season. By deciding to stay in the Pac-10, attending OSU would allow me the opportunity to show the Bears of Cal their error in not recruiting me aggressively. I'll share with you later how much I particularly enjoyed OSU's game against Cal in my junior season.

I'll never forget the day I left for college. I had all my things packed and ready to go. I got up early to say my good-byes, called all of the relatives who helped mold my existence positively and all my friends. On the way to the airport with my family, I knew it was going to be a long time before I came back. I was planning to be on my own to make my own decisions and be responsible for myself.

Being responsible for myself may not seem like a lofty goal, but it is. It means taking responsibility for your future, taking your future in your own hands. You have the power to mold your future, to make yourself a pro, if you want to bad enough. I know I'm no Michael Jordan or even a Terrell Davis, but I have enjoyed the friendship of people like Derrick Thomas, Marcus Allen, Joe Montana, Neil Smith, Christian Okoye, Andre Rison, Reggie White and many, many more. I have earned the right to wear the NFL insignia and patch on my jersey. All that grows out of my decision to be responsible for myself, the decision I made on the day I left home for college.

I have met some wonderful people through the years and also endured terrible experiences that have motivated me to work harder than anyone around me, I overcame all the roadblocks and all the negative energy people threw at me to bring me down. I made it, and I have been able to play for almost ten years as a professional football player in the NFL and the World League. But I paid my dues.

So, You Want to be a Pro?

I think this book will help you learn how to pay your dues. I hope you read every word because I have a very important story to tell. When I say "professional," it doesn't mean just a professional football player, hockey player or baseball player. The word *professional* encompasses a whole scope of definitions.

The most important thing I want you to take from this book is a sense of confidence that you can become anything you want to become. Overcoming obstacles and creating opportunities is a function of desire. You can build a long-lasting foundation for success based on hard work and discipline. Most of all, you can create the desire to become anything you dream of with the right attitude and plan.

Becoming a pro is a road filled with pitfalls and obstacles, a road traveled alone at times. You will have to sacrifice to realize your dream. In the process, you will set the standards by which you will live the rest of your life.

So, you want to be a pro? Do you think you have what it takes? I'm not talking about the moves, or the jumpshot or the curve ball. Do you have the **attitude?** Do you have the **discipline?** Do you have the **commitment?**

- Nothing is more important than a great **attitude.** With a great attitude, you can't fail at finding your dreams. And, you will draw other people to your side who like your attitude and want to be part of your victorious outlook.

- **Discipline** is the way you translate your attitude into action. Discipline means waking up in the morning in time to succeed. It means taking care of the simplest details, making the right choices under pressure.

• The strength of your attitude and your discipline together, tells people what **commitment** you have to becoming a pro. Measure your commitment to this dream you are planning to pursue and find out if you really have what it takes. Look at failure as a learning opportunity, not an obstacle. Determine what a leader is and develop the skills to be one, to be able to stand up to your peers. Commit to making your body the tool you need to get this professional job done. Commit to making your mind the sharpest, most ready part of your body, aimed at nothing but success.

Attitude

Attitude is defined by *Webster's Dictionary* as:

1. *A bodily posture showing mood, action, etc.* 2. *A manner showing one's feeling or thoughts.* 3. *One's disposition, opinion, etc.*

When the coach singles you out and asks you to perform a certain technique, how do you react? Are you willing? Are you enthused? Do you care who's watching? Do you care what your teammates think? Your answer to these questions determines your attitude.

Your attitude demonstrates how you react to changes and challenges. Others will gain insight to your *inner* self by your *outer* behavior - your attitude, your demeanor, the way you carry yourself. A sign posted on many locker room walls says your attitude will determine your altitude. A positive attitude will help you climb high and achieve seemingly unreachable goals. Conversely, a negative attitude will ground you and keep you from ever recognizing your potential and the potential of others around you.

The great thing about attitude is you have the choice. It's up to you. You have to decide a positive attitude is what you carry. Once you have made the decision, you must work at it. Every day, every hour, every minute you must work at it until being positive becomes a part of who you are.

Remember the stories I told you about my life growing up. I told you those stories for a reason. They show you how easy it would have been for me to simply sink into a negative attitude. Just about everything in my life seemed to be going against me. I could easily have given up and my dreams would have been grounded. But I didn't. I chose to have a positive attitude. I *willed* a positive attitude just as you *will* yourself to finish that last wind sprint. And, my positive attitude prevailed.

From reading this book, you know where I've been. You know what my early years were like. I turned those negatives into positives, those hurts into energy. I showed 'em.

If I can, you can too.

Here's how:

- *When someone says something negative, respond positively regardless of what they say.* It's hard to do because the first thing you want to do is make the person shut up and leave you alone. But, in the real world, you can't always control your environment. You may know what is around you and know what to expect, but you can't control it. As a professional athlete, you cannot respond to some heckler in the stands because he makes a comment about your jump shot or how you field the ball. By saying something negative, you lose that opportunity to focus on what you want out of life and what you have worked so hard to pursue.

- *Remember what your goals are.* There will always be people who don't want you to succeed because of jealousy and envy. Don't lower yourself to their level if you want to be successful. Keep your attitude positive.

- *Don't let defeat stop you.* All of us know who the greatest basketball player in the NBA was. Would you believe he got cut from his high school basketball team twice? That's right, His Airness, Michael Jordan, at one time in his life, *wasn't good enough.* Can you tell me why all of us know who he is? Because he didn't stop trying. He committed himself and kept his attitude positive. He practiced and made himself better by shooting baskets every day until he finally got his chance. What about Steve Largent - former NFL star and current congressman? What about Steve Kerr, former Arizona standout and current NBA star? How did they feel when they were told they were too small or too slow to play? What do you think got them motivated to try harder? The school bully chasing them every day before practice? No, a positive attitude.

- *Believe in yourself no matter what anybody says.* You know all about Michael Jordan, Steve Largent and Steve Kerr. How about Dennis Smith? Do you know who he is? Of course not; he gave up after eighth grade when another kid said he was too fat to play football. Where is Dennis today? Who knows? He believed what the other kids said about him, not what he believed about himself.

And he's probably still fat, I hope not though!

A positive attitude will give you all the confidence you need to set out on your journey called "Success." A negative attitude will only sink your dreams before they have a chance to blossom. Repeat these lines out loud: "I can, I will, I must have a positive attitude. With a positive attitude, I can and will do great things." Now say it again and again until you believe it. A positive attitude will help you do your best no matter what the circumstances. You will always find the silver lining in every situation.

When I was willing to set aside my career with Procter & Gamble for an outside shot at pro football, the starting point had to be my attitude. I wasn't going to be denied.

At the World League tryout held at Sacramento State, which was the first step to squeezing myself into an opportunity to play professional football, I was an uninvited lightweight at 250 pounds with a pair of red baseball shoes to run in. They were the only shoes I could find that would fit and were affordable at a local sporting goods store. They only cost me $10, and they made me look fast.

Because I was without an invitation, it was hard to be acknowledged. Anyone who showed up without their name on the list couldn't work out. I had to sit in the bleachers and watch the rest of the athletes go through warm-ups and stretches. I had to sit as they ran 40s. As the tryout was close to concluding, I had the feeling that my dream was getting farther and farther out of reach. At the last minute, they called the rest of us over to run a couple of drills. Now, after watching everyone run and jump, skip and stretch, I was ready to run through a brick wall. *Whatever it took to make an impression, to get a chance, I was going to do.*

Chet Franklin, now the vice-president of operations for the New Orleans Saints, ran a drill for defensive linemen. His instructions were simple: run through the cones and sprint to him. That was easy enough, so when my turn came I attacked the cones and tried to run through him. After he gave us a variation, I again attacked the cones and went after him. Then he looked at me and smiled slightly. I think he knew I was hungry and the tryout was important to me. After two or three more times through, the drilling was over. It was all or nothing and I felt I made the best of my opportunity. I prayed it was good enough. I walked over to the infield where I gathered my shoes and sweatshirt, then sat to cool down and stretch. One of the camp coordinators came to talk to me.

He asked me my name again and paused as if he was trying to put two-and-two together. I told him who I was, where I went to school and what I had been doing until that tryout, that I was then working for Procter & Gamble. He explained to me what was to happen at the next event, if I was invited to the combine in Orlando, Florida. As he was leaving, I had the feeling I had a pretty good chance at being invited to participate in the World League draft. Keep in mind, I also thought I was going to be an NFL draft pick and you know that story. All I could do was pray. And pray I did. Prayer helps. A positive attitude helps, too.

How to have a positive attitude

You can develop a positive attitude if you want to. But it takes great effort and mental toughness.

1. Make the decision. I can. I will. I must have a positive attitude.

2. Find out what makes you special. What do you bring to the table?

3. Focus on your strengths.

4. Never make excuses. Know your priorities.

5. Don't take failure personally. Accept each opportunity to grow.

6. Don't be afraid to succeed. Be confident.

These six mental strategies will help you tap the positive attitude within you, which will help you on your journey.

Discipline

The word discipline has many meanings and different circumstances in which it is applied. *Webster's Dictionary* defines discipline as:

1. *Training that develops self-control, efficiency, etc.* 2. *Strict control to enforce obedience.* 3. *Orderly conduct.* 4. *A system of rules.* 5. *Treatment that corrects or punishes.*

As you develop your positive attitude, you will find it takes great effort to consistently think positive thoughts in times of duress. Focusing on your strengths as opposed to your weaknesses is not easy. Don't make excuses. Continue, despite failure, and be confident. That's where discipline comes in.

It will be discipline that helps keep your focus on your target when your friends are partying, or doing something that seems a lot more fun than homework. Because of your commitment to your goal, take a pass on the partying. It will be your discipline that will help you to decide your future, and that's more important than any destructive behavior your peers may be involved in. When it's time to get ready for the BIG GAME, and some of your friends would rather do something else the night before, you'll make the right decision because the team needs you.

Your discipline and commitment to the team could pay large dividends. Who knows? You could get your big chance at any time. Being prepared to play (in sports, business and life) gives you every opportunity to be successful. You never know, it could be you who scores the game-winning touchdown run, because you stayed home and studied your plays that much more. And who's to say if there's a recruiter in the stands from Notre Dame or UCLA watching another kid? Guess who showed up to play? Maybe the one who is best prepared to play will catch his eye.

I can relate to that story well. When I was a senior in high school, I was running out of opportunities to impress a Division I-A school like Cal or Oklahoma. The last game of the season was against a team that all but dominated the league in every sport. Their best athlete was a guy by the name of Tim Ryan. Tim and I played against each other a total of four games. On that day, my coaches told me scouts would be out looking at Ryan. I thought, "Why shouldn't I take advantage of the attention he was getting?" I played offense and defense, so I had an opportunity to show my stuff against him going both ways.

We had the ball first and, as soon as I put my hand on the ground, Tim lined up in front of me. *"I'm going to make you eat your lunch."* That's what he said to me. My response was, *"Bring it on."* It was a great day to compete and we did. I don't know how much that game impacted my scholarship chances. All I know is my coaches were proud of the fact that I went out and competed with pride against a *Parade Magazine* All-American who had a full ride to USC.

The word discipline has many meanings and it is applied in many different circumstances. To me, discipline means doing what is supposed to be done all of the time, not just when someone is watching. *All the time.* There are many ways for young aspiring athletes to apply the word discipline to their lives. The biggest is a steady study habit. That's right, study habit.

Here's one where good study habits pay off in sports. How many times has your coach told you to go home and study your playbook and then given you a new play that you've never seen before? Maybe your coach gave it to you at halftime or on the bench during a timeout. In any event, you had to be prepared to learn on the spot. Practicing good study habits will allow you to learn the play quickly because you have practiced breaking down problems to understand them. There are a lot of athletes who are just that, athletes. It takes a special person to be a scholar-athlete. Good study habits help make you a smart athlete.

Not everyone is strong or fast and not every athlete is a rocket scientist. To separate yourself from the pack, improve your study habits in the classroom and those habits will carry over into your athletics. Being a smart athlete creates several advantages for you. Ask Michael Jordan or Cowboy quarterback Troy Aikman. They study the game - they know their opponents. By using good study habits, you can learn the little things that make the difference between winning and losing. Outthinking your opponent and being able to anticipate a play before it happens can be crucial to victory. By being disciplined, you will give yourself a greater chance at being successful by giving yourself more opportunities to be successful.

What are study habits? Many students do not read textbook material well, if at all. Successful students, however, usually read text material more than once. Think about reading ahead as preparation for the first exam. It may help you to take the reading more seriously and get more out of it.

Read the introduction and summary first, then outline the main points covered in the summary. You should have a pretty good idea of the chapter's general content. (Source: Center for Personal and Professional Development)

Some successful students read everything in the chapter that's set in bold face type first, just skimming through picking out all the subheads and captions and chapter titles. It doesn't take long, but it prepares you to understand. It's like understanding the game plan of the chapter; once you know the strategy, the rest makes more sense.

After you've prepared this way, you are now ready to actually read. Try to think like a teacher as you read, coming up with possible test questions based on the content of the summary and chapter, asking yourself, "What would I want the student to know here?"

Commitment

Webster's Dictionary defines commitment as:

1. *Committing or being committed.* 2. *A pledge or promise to do something.* 3. *Dedication to a long-term course of action.*

By now, you know the values of a positive attitude and discipline. Now you need to know that to achieve the goal you have set high on the mantle requires a great deal of sacrifice. The one component that ties attitude and discipline together is commitment.

It's simple. If you want to play on the high school football team, you must show up to practice, meetings and other events required by the team. If you have a job and the boss requires you to arrive at a certain time, you should be early or at least on time. In both cases, if you do not show up and, more importantly, if you do not follow the rules, or you abuse the rules, you can and will be cut or fired.

Commitment is a strong word and an important one if you want to be a professional athlete. When you commit to something, you have dedicated yourself to seeing the project through. It also means establishing priorities that will put you in a position to take advantage of all of your opportunities when they arise and create those you need to succeed. A common result of this commitment is the development of strong character. Remember this! Becoming a person of character is a far greater accomplishment than even becoming a professional athlete.

Character

What is character? The *American Heritage Dictionary* defines character as:

1. *The combination of qualities or features that distinguishes one person, group, or thing from another.* 2. *A distinguishing feature or attribute, as of an individual, a group, or a category.*

Who we are is defined by our actions not only in front of people, but also when no one is watching. The things you do today will most likely affect you tomorrow. Each action, positive or negative, good or bad, helps create who you are. Your character is tested every day. Have you ever been in a situation in which someone has entrusted you to complete a project and left you there to complete it on your own? Maybe your teacher left the room during a test or quiz, your coach ran to the locker room during drills or one of your parents went to the store while you were doing homework. These people have given you a job to complete and you have to make a decision on whether or not to complete it. Your character will be revealed by what you do when they are gone.

Obstacles

One of the greatest fears we have as human beings is the fear of failure. Unexpected obstacles along the way breed failure. We have been conditioned by society and, in most cases, our parents, to look at failure in a shameful way. "You didn't do your best," or, "Can't you do anything right?" are phrases heard by individuals your age (mine too, for that matter) every day. From a statistical point of view, failure is not a positive experience to 99 percent of all individuals. When criticized by peers and co-workers, they are embarrassed by lack of success. But what about that 1 percent? One person in a hundred looks at failure as an opportunity to learn, a chance to weed out the possibilities to find the answer. That one person in a hundred grows from obstacles.

Only one kind of failure is real. That's the failure to pursue a dream with passion regardless of what others think. Before Thomas Edison perfected the light bulb he experimented with lots of different filaments. He failed hundreds of times before he found the right element to make his dream a reality. What you need to do is find the element of support to make your dream a reality.

As a young person in this world, your peers become very critical of all your pursuits and frequently judge everything you do. Your misfortunes become an amusement to them. They laugh when you fall and tease when you stumble, but as soon as you stand on top of the hill, they'll be there to hold you high upon their shoulders. Why, you ask? Because they are looking for someone to follow, someone to be a leader. If you fall and get up, they can only laugh at the fall. If you fall and don't get up, they can laugh at you. The act of falling may not have been your fault, but the decision to get up is all on you.

Injuries are a prime example of your being faultless in the act of falling. Everyone knows injuries happen. I know from first-hand experience. At Oregon State, we had a freshmen team that played local junior colleges and small universities. It was good for our freshmen class. Although my chance to play anywhere above the freshman level was very limited, my enthusiasm stayed high because I knew I would have my chance someday. I continued my attempt to break into the varsity lineup as a freshman, but fate would have it another way. In a game against Eastern Washington, I took a shot to my right knee that tore it up pretty good. Just like that, my season was over and I hardly got the chance to play. The only thing I had to look forward to was a cast for six weeks and watching my teammates enjoy the season.

Sometimes, I think about that injury and see it as an awakening. When I got hurt, my eyes opened up and I realized I might not have a future in football. It was time to start thinking about the importance of my education. What did I want to do with my life? I was alone and unsure of myself.

When a high school senior goes off to college, the expectation going through his or her head is one of grand accomplishments. In my case, I visualized one day standing at the entrance of a tunnel leading to a stadium filled with adoring NFL fans. But after my injury, my dreams of playing professional football were all but gone. I was depressed for a month and I tried to figure out what to do next.

I didn't have anyone to talk to about what went on and how I felt. I thought about going back home or transferring to a different university. I thought about going to a black college like Howard

So, You Want to be a Pro?

University or Morehouse College because those were probably better for me, at least socially. OSU had a .01 percent population of black students on campus and, after awhile, the fresh air and beautiful trees didn't matter. I found myself searching for reasons to stay. I knew I'd lose my scholarship, but I wanted to get away. Right away.

Why could I feel that way? I was in a situation most 18-year-olds yearn for and I thought about quitting. I never had quit anything before, so why did I consider it at that time? Most people would find a way out because things weren't going their way and I felt like I was one of them. I thought about running away from a small setback and giving up the scholarship I had worked so hard to get. Then one day, I woke up. I realized what I was doing. I was trying to find an acceptable reason to justify leaving school. I didn't want to leave; so I had to use the situation. So what if I didn't play football anymore? I still had my scholarship, which meant my schooling was paid for. I had the chance to pursue any dream I wanted. I didn't have to wait for an opportunity. It was in front of me and I saw it.

I also saw that I couldn't let it matter I was on a predominately white campus because that's the way it is in the real world. I learned to cut my own hair because it was cheaper. Plus, after I got real good at it, I was able to make some spare change. The choice was clear: Would I make that situation positive or negative? I chose the positive. I told myself, "Right now is the time that you have to be the strongest. This is what real life is all about and no one is going to give me anything. I'm going to work for it and take it if I must."

Another circumstance that is out of your control, but can prove to be an obstacle, is a change in coaching. When the summer started before my senior year in college, I did my running and lifting at the stadium in the afternoon, then watched an hour of film before heading home. I ran by Dave Tipton's office to talk about techniques and got advice when I needed it. Tipton was defensive line coach. He was my new mentor and I was his student. One day when I was working out in the stadium, Coach Tipton came out as he usually did if he saw me out there. That day, he had some good news and some bad. The good news was that he had been offered a job at Stanford; the bad news, he was leaving at the end of the week to start coaching. I was crushed. I didn't tell him, but at the time I felt betrayed and angry at the world. He had helped me blossom into the football player and person I am. His trust and confidence in me helped me in my success.

I started to lose my focus because I felt betrayed, but I came around after a couple of days and got back after it and tried even harder to be as perfect as possible. My mentor was leaving, but he had given me the knowledge and know-how and it was time I used it. It wasn't easy. Within two weeks, another defensive line coach was in his office. On coaching, I got a first-hand look at the business in which the only thing constant is change. It happens at all levels.

With Coach Tipton, it was at the college level. Later, many things popped up in my professional days that were just out of my hands. The point is, it *is* easy to worry about those things. And also a waste of time.

During the entire 1991 season, every player on my World League team anticipated the chance of getting an NFL tryout. Almost every day I would look through the sports section of the newspaper to see who was picked up by an NFL team. And almost every day I felt bad because I wasn't one of the lucky souls to get the chance to take that next step. Occasionally I recognized one or two guys whose names appeared in small letters under the transactions column and I found myself putting them down. When you get down to it, I was discrediting them while trying to convince myself I deserved more of a shot. Then I would feel terrible because I had lost my focus. I knew one day I would have my chance, but I had to earn it.

My head coach in Birmingham in 1991 and 1992 was Chan Gailey who ultimately got his first NFL head coaching job with the Dallas Cowboys. He received a couple of phone calls from two different NFL teams interested in me, the Philadelphia Eagles and the New Orleans Saints.

Training camp didn't go as well as I hoped with the Eagles because I hardly had a chance to play. When I did, it was in the closing minutes of an exhibition game. Although out of my control, it was more embarrassing than anything else. I thought I should have been playing for at least a half, but the head coach felt otherwise so I sat on the bench. Finally, I got tired of playing in the fading minutes of the exhibition games and got the nerve up to ask for my release. I couldn't stand it, so I asked to be let go so I could go back to Portland to start graduate school. Although the situation was very frustrating, it taught me a valuable lesson that every opportunity is a chance to learn. I learned to deal with the disappointment of being so close to my dream, yet being so far because I was denied the chance to truly participate. Although the Philadelphia situation was out of my control, I felt my goal was within striking distance.

I was going to make it. Maybe not at that time, but my time was near.

When I got back to Portland, I took a job as a defensive line coach for a local high school varsity football team and also assisted with the junior varsity team. Although it was frustrating being away from playing the entire NFL season, I enjoyed teaching the young aspiring professionals some of the lessons I had learned in the short period of time I played. Between trying to find a job, going back to school and coaching, I was anticipating the opportunity to get back to Birmingham. The 1992 World League season ended like the 1991 season. We had another outstanding year but lost in the playoffs to the Orlando Thunder.

Only this time something interesting happened after the game. An NFL scout came up to me and asked if I would be interested in coming to Kansas City as a free agent. I was in shock. I couldn't believe I was actually getting the chance that I prayed for. Once I was on the bus, all I could do was smile. We finished the playoff game on Sunday and by the following Tuesday night I was in Kansas City. I was ready to make my mark on the organization and the NFL. I had gotten a second chance because I didn't let a very big obstacle stop me.

Again, I was faced with a situation out of my control, but it sure whetted my appetite.

Leap That Hurdle and Get Ready for the Next One

Attitude, discipline and commitment. I used all three when I got my opportunity with the Chiefs. When I came to the home of the Chiefs in 1992, I knew I had the chance of a lifetime. Unlike the Eagles, I felt that I had a legitimate opportunity to become a part of one of the premier organizations in the NFL. I joined the team toward the end of the off-season workout programs as a defensive end. After the World League season, I was down to around 260 pounds, which meant I needed to gain some weight to be able to play for the Chiefs. I started lifting and learned the defense as best as I could. On special teams, I learned how to play several positions like guard and tackle on the punt team, wedge tackle on the kick-off return team, and anything else I could convince the special teams coach to let me try.

I went through training camp confident of my ability to make the team. I was very detailed in everything that was asked of me and in my performance. On the practice field, I tried to be the first one at every drill and perform them almost to perfection. I was persistent and wasn't going to be denied the chance to make it. After five weeks of training camp, we were prepared to play the last game of the exhibition season. I survived two cuts during camp and figured to lay it on the line for the Monday night match-up between the Chiefs and the Buffalo Bills.

As I stood at the opening of the elephant tunnel (opening to the field) and looked into the sea of red at Arrowhead Stadium, I was ready. I felt my heart pound deep within my chest. Every beat became an impulse of anticipation to run on the field between the row of cheerleaders. I could see myself on the big screen in the stadium, poised in front the entire world as a professional athlete and member of the Kansas City Chiefs.

Because it was the last exhibition game, the starters played the first couple of series, then the second team played until the end of the first half. I was third on the depth chart, which meant I waited until the second half to play.

"Put me in, coach, I'm ready to play now," I thought to myself. I walked up and down the sideline during the first half of the game. This was my last chance to make the team. When the first half ended, I felt the butterflies starting to spread their wings in my stomach.

When we came out of the locker room for the second half, I was less than ninety minutes away from my dream, I thought. In that half, I made four tackles with a couple of quarterback pressures. I also covered punts on the punt team and was on the kickoff return team. We won, 35-3, and I thought I had done it. All the work, all the sacrifices, all the pain and I had finally done it. No more doubts of my ability, no more player haters telling me that I wasn't good enough to make it.

On Tuesday, Mark Hatley, the director of pro personnel at the time, called me on the phone and told me the team was going to release me. For a minute I was in shock. I didn't expect it, although I was prepared for the possibility.

Talk about the ultimate tease! Feeling that atmosphere at Arrowhead and playing well enough to land a spot on the roster. At least I thought I played well enough.

The Chiefs did, however, sign me as a developmental player. I was disappointed, of course, but I still had an opportunity to play in the NFL. Who knew what the possibilities would be? I didn't, but I was going to take advantage of it. As a developmental player, I did everything but play in the game. It was a good experience because it gave me a real taste of being a part of a team. It lasted for close to six weeks before they released me because of injuries. They needed another player at a different position.

Extremely displeased, I went back to Oregon feeling rejected and depressed. I worked hard for two World League seasons, sacrificing, being very disciplined, making all the right decisions, and I was still without a job. I saved enough money to survive for about three months, but I had to find a job to be able to live. I started selling long distance telephone service during the day and I worked as a bouncer at night.

In February of 1993, after receiving a letter from the Chiefs inviting me back, I left Oregon and haven't looked back since. Now I can say that it was all worth the effort. Every minute, every sacrifice, every cold bowl of noodles led to a roster spot on an NFL team. Every bit of it made me appreciate all that I have become.

While thinking about overcoming obstacles and failures, keep in mind that one of the greatest baseball players of all time, George Brett, had a lifetime batting average of .305. Do you know what that really means? It means he hit safely in three out of every ten at-bats and FAILED the seven other times. By the average person's standard, George Brett was a failure. His ability to hit became the driving force behind the Kansas City Royals' success during his 20-year career. And don't think for a moment he didn't have his own obstacles to overcome. Despite injuries that hampered him throughout his career, Brett still managed to reach the magical 3,000-hit plateau. In 1980, Brett batted .390, the highest batting average in Major League Baseball since Ted Williams hit .406 in 1941 with the Boston Red Sox, but injuries limited him to 117 games played that year. On Jan. 5, 1999, he was elected to Baseball's Hall of Fame. Brett's hard-working attitude, discipline and commitment to be the best elevated him to icon status.

So, if you fall, stand up and smile, then try again. If you continue to fall, step back and evaluate your situation. Use others' sarcasm as motivation to pursue your dream. Little do they realize there are people out there who become exceptional individuals because they continue to try regardless of criticism. In fact, they feed on criticism. They use it to get stronger.

If you combine the big three - attitude, discipline, and commitment - you can meet any obstacles and run right through it. Life *will* place obstacles in your path, just the way football offenses place three-hundred-pound linemen in your path. Run around them or run through them, but don't let them keep you from the prize.

Expectations

Contemporary college athletes experience tremendous pressure. Not only do you compete on the athletic field, you compete in the classroom. High school scholar-athletes experience even more pressure as soon as they sign a letter of intent. If you are in the top 10 percent of the athletes in your sport, there is a mountain of expectations you have just assumed. There are many ways to meet the challenge of those expectations, some good and some bad. Here, we will only emphasize the good.

For a gifted young athlete, the expectation of going off to college to become the next Grant Hill, Peyton Manning or Tiger Woods is a reality. The pressure is felt at home, at school, in the community and in the media. Before you have the chance to play your first snap in football, people are pulling you in every direction imaginable. The one thing that will save you is the expectation you have for yourself and how you have set it up.

Setting expectations for your future is a goal-setting process we have talked about under commitment. The difference between your personal goals, or dreams, and the goals you set when you sign a letter or intent for college is that you are obligated to other people now and they have expectations for you. One way to make it easier on yourself is, to find out exactly what their expectations are before you choose to attend that particular college. If their expectations for you are lower than your own, then you have to make a choice if it is in your best interest to attend. Universities strive to provide a clear explanation of their expectations of potential student-athletes and you should do the same. The university has an obligation to provide an atmosphere that is positive to the growth of the student-athlete, academically and athletically. Student-athletes have a responsibility to fulfill expectations as part of their entrance into the university. These expectations include:

1. Meeting all academic responsibilities.

2. Being part of the university culture.

3. Understanding and utilizing the support services available.

4. Recognizing that earning a degree is a personal responsibility.

5. Understanding that you represent your family, the university and the athletic department at all times.

If you are willing to accept these expectations and work toward the goals you set for yourself, as well as those set by the university, the university will find every way to ensure you graduate with a degree and have a clear career path. But that's not enough. Ultimately, the responsibility of succeeding in college is on you. It's up to you to handle the responsibility of being on a college campus, to evaluate yourself and your actions, to listen and work with others and, lastly, to set goals and evaluate your options. Those decisions will determine the quality of your collegiate career.

Responsibility

The discipline needed to be a student-athlete is time consuming. Academic survival and growth of the student-athlete is an ongoing evaluation that is monitored by the athletic department and the university. Adequate progress towards a degree will bring recognition and honors. The university and athletic department standards will evaluate inadequate progress strictly. Failure to meet the university requirements and, most importantly, the National Collegiate Athletic Association's eligibility standards could render you ineligible for competition. You could also lose your scholarship if you fail to regain your eligibility.

No matter what you think or may have been told, this is not an area where your athletic prowess will save the day. NCAA and NAIA rules about eligibility are pretty clear and exceptionally strict. Try telling the NCAA you slept through the final because your roommate kept you up all night or you didn't do the homework because you had practice all afternoon. You have just met an immovable object, maybe even the first authority you haven't been able to move with your fancy footwork. Absolutely no substitute exists for academic success when it comes to the NCAA, or the NAIA. Those organizations set the bar for academic success and you have to meet it.

They don't, however, set the bar very high. Just because you meet their standards, doesn't mean you will graduate. Some athletes make the huge mistake of enrolling only in the minimum hours for eligibility, not the number they need to graduate in four years, or enrolling in only the easiest courses, not the specific courses they need to fulfill a major. That's a big waste of a genuine opportunity, your athletic scholarship. Your scholarship can be your ticket to a better life, even if you fail to make the pros. And remember, statistically speaking, you are probably not going to make it to the pros. But if you make good use of your scholarship, you can become a pro of another sort - a professional lawyer or a professional doctor, or an accountant or business manager, an entrepreneur, inventor, commentator. You have a responsibility to succeed, no matter what.

There is an extreme amount of pressure to perform in all phases of the phenomenon known as the student-athlete. You must work hard in and out of uniform. Are you up to the challenge? Are you sure you want to pursue the unknown?

Big Obstacles You Put in Your Own Way

In the world of professional athletics, it is always possible to find a horror story about a player starting out with what seems like all the money in the world and ending up with nothing. Those same horror stories, maybe without all the money, are found on your level, too. Instead, it may be in the form of athletic ability, the kind that can be your meal ticket if you play your cards right or lost entirely if you don't.

Alcohol, drugs and other compromising scenarios are usually found at the root of many of these stories. Players involved with these vices are set up for potential embarrassment, incarceration, or even worse, death. Stories such as these cause pain to many people including college administrators, team management, family members and friends. The lifestyle we choose is shown in our environment and the individuals with whom we choose to associate. The people we choose to have around us, how we carry ourselves in the public eye, how we treat those who support us and how we exercise common sense, make up our "lifestyle."

Some people think their lifestyle is the clothes they wear, the cars they drive, the music they listen to, the tattoo on their biceps. Your lifestyle is much deeper than that. It is the display of your character and your character determines whether you will fail or succeed in life and in sports.

In your daily life and throughout your career, there will be many expectations you must try to meet. More important will be the expectations we have for ourselves, directed at being successful as an individual and fulfilling personal goals. You and the organization must share the same vision as it relates to expectations. As a professional, it is your responsibility to educate yourself about the environment in which you work. The organization has goals, too, but the most positive thing you can do as a professional is set personal expectations that will, without a doubt, help the team accomplish what it sets out to do. To be a professional means to carry yourself on and off the field like you mean business, as if "all eyes are on me." Simply put, "Act like a professional; get treated like one." The expectations of a team to its players is simple. Carry yourself in the public eye as a professional and a representative of the organization in which you work.

That type of conduct starts with where you are now. Though you aren't paid, you are still representing your school outside your playing arena. Remember, you chose to play your sport in high school or college and the coach chose you to be a part of that particular team. It is a privilege to be chosen. Others would trade places with you if they had the same abilities. When you're not wearing your uniform, you are still accountable for your actions because of the privilege of being included on a team. Like it or not, that's the bottom line.

You'll also find that family and friends have varying expectations. If you make it professionally, some family members believe that, because you made it, you owe everyone you grew up with. Other family members expect you to be their own personal bank. Take it from someone who has been asked the same questions you will be asked. Unless there is a dire situation in which your help is desperately needed, you must learn to say no. You have good reason.

Did you know that the average NFL career is about 3.2 years long and not much longer in the other major sports? Imagine spending four years of high school dedicating yourself to your sport, then another four years of college, and actually have less than four years to compete professionally. Logically, think what would happen if you gave up most of your money to family and relatives your first year in the league. What would happen if you got hurt? Could you get the money back if you needed it? Would they be available to you? Family is important, but don't forget about your future.

Outside your family, the community in which you play also has high expectations of you. They support your on-the-field endeavors by buying tickets, replicas of your jersey and other events surrounding the organization you represent. In return, they want to see you in the community. This might involve playing with their children, visiting homes for the elderly and sick, helping rebuild their lives or just showing them in some way you appreciate all of their support. Your community is very important to the development of your communication, business and overall people skills. Remember, people support what they help create.

You may get a taste of community involvement on the college level because of the increasing number of programs that athletic departments are starting across the country. For groups like Special Olympics, you and your teammates may be asked to participate in voluntary clinics. The pros may seem so far away, but some of your actions in community involvement are right around the corner.

Performance and Perception

Most see professional sports as something that anyone can participate in if they are capable of catching a football or shooting a basket. They are sadly mistaken. The time it takes to prepare for one game is something a person outside of athletics wouldn't understand. Players dedicate their lives to becoming the best professional athlete they can be and deserve what they earn. A lot of sacrifice, discipline and time is involved. As long as people are interested in pro sports, those who are willing to sacrifice to be the best will, and should, benefit.

By choosing this profession you leave yourself open to a lot of criticism from the media, the general public, and the fans who fill the stands. Many perceptions will dictate how every fan will see you, but there is a reality to those perceptions. Here are a few of them.

Perception: The world of professional athletics is a world of easy living and can't be real work. It's too much fun.

Reality: The dedication needed to perform as a professional is time-consuming and laborious. Between workouts, film study, practice and your obligation to your family, there is no time to sit back and enjoy all that you have accomplished. Someone is always trying to take your job or pay you less. Most of the fun you have is in performing on your game day.

Perception: Players are overpaid.

Reality: Professional athletes are entertainers. If you go to see Clint Eastwood in a movie, you go because you like him, don't you? He entertains you with his talent as an actor. So why is it so hard to pay a professional athlete? A professional athlete is performing the same as an actor. Both practice and prepare, both invest enormous amounts of time in giving the best performance they possibly can. Actors like Clint Eastwood enjoy large box office success and no one complains.

So, You Want to be a Pro?

Perception: Some fans assume they pay your entire salary and that gives them the right to criticize all that you do.

Reality: Anyone who buys a ticket, or a shirt with your team logo or insignia pays some of your salary. Although relatively small, that amount does contribute to your salary, but it ends there. People may be critical of you regardless of what you do in the community. The choices you make should be influenced by the fact you still represent the organization and the community in which you work. Not what fans believe what you should do.

Perception: No one cares about the fans who occupy the stadiums and arenas.

Reality: Thanks to fans, the business of professional sports generates billions of dollars each year. The owners of sports teams, the cities in which they play, the vendors who sell concessions, as well as the players benefit from this support.

If you are good enough to become a professional athlete, what you do with your personal time is no longer private, especially if you want the success of a superstar. Companies which have a stake in promoting and endorsing professional and amateur athletes will only accept 100 percent compliance if you want the opportunity to endorse their product. Athletes who have very public problems are bad for business and corporations are not in the business of losing money. How people see you as a person will dictate the number of opportunities you will get and those you will lose or never see.

Check yourself

Carry yourself like a professional all the time and you will feel like one in time.

Chapter 5
A dual path strategy

Making a choice

The choice to pursue a career in professional athletics is easy, but choosing a realistic career is sometimes a very difficult and life changing decision. The balance of what is desired and what is realistic is a difficult pill to swallow, but sooner or later you will have no choice. Selecting the right career path that will allow you to transition from student-athlete to student or student-athlete to salesman can be very difficult, but it doesn't have to be.

While you are in high school, college and even professional athletics, it is important that you keep a clear understanding, that sports as a profession is temporary. If you couldn't play your chosen sport tomorrow or any sport ever again what would you do? Would you attend a vocational school to learn a trade? Would you live at home with your parents until they kicked you out? Would you work for minimum wage at a burger joint 60 hours a week? Seriously, what would you do?

These types of questions are the same ones I asked myself in college. What did I want to do if and when I couldn't play football anymore? Did I want to have nothing to show for all my hard work, but broken bones, scars and memories of being a college football player? No, not me. I wanted more. I wanted to achieve great things. I wanted to travel around the world and see it with my own eyes. I wanted to be able to live in my own home and drive my own car. I wanted the responsibility of being an adult.

Thinking about your future before it presents itself is so very important to your success as an individual. The only thing that you need to do is decide that it is worth preparing for.

How do you select that next career? I often ask individuals this question, "When do you feel free?" By that I mean, what makes you feel that you are on top of the world and no one can stop you. It could be when you are writing, painting, singing, fixing a car, creating a science fair project or serving humanity. It could be one of these things or none of these things, but as long as it has positive impact on you and society your choices are vast. By creating a dual path you will enable yourself the chance to be successful. Adults will tell you, "starting a new career, adjusting to job changes and job losses is a very frustrating and emotional ordeal." The stability and security of any job has all but disappeared. You are in charge of your professional development experiences. You are in charge of your own career, managing it will be a lifelong process.

By finding your place in the world outside of athletics you will be able to enjoy a level of satisfaction that will focus on your own unique skills, knowledge, personality and interests. You will be able to balance the important relationships and make decisions that will be beneficial. To make this a reality, it is important to research your career options. It may sound silly, but in order to be successful in any field you have got to know what you are doing.

Setting up your plan

By creating a plan, you give yourself the best chance to make the transition an exciting one, but it takes preparation.

Visualize your success! Take the time to focus on the steps you'll need to take to accomplish your goal.

Set long-term goals! If you are a baseball player and you would like to be an accomplished artist, research and find out what it takes to survive in such a competitive profession. You already have the skills, now map out how to apply them.

Get experience! Summer jobs and internships can expose you to potential careers. It can also give you the work experience employers are looking for in new employees.

In addition, if you should choose to pursue some degree of higher education, it will allow you to climb the corporate ladder a lot more smoothly. All these things make up a plan of action that will allow you to maximize your opportunities for success.

What is a resumé?

Make a positive first impression. A resumé will give a prospective employer all the information they need to make a decision about hiring you. The document should include your name, telephone number and complete address. Put the most important information near the top where it will be easy to find. Your work experience should go first and list the jobs you've held beginning with the most recent. If you don't have any work experience be sure to write how much you would enjoy the opportunity to have the experience. Your education should be next. List school(s) and degrees in your education section with dates. If you are in high school, write what college you plan to attend and when. You never know what can happen, it's possible that you may be setting up a future summer job or internship. Lastly, include a cover letter with your resumé.

What is a cover letter? A cover letter tells the employer exactly what kind of job you want and gives an introduction to who you are. A well-written cover letter will state your professional objectives, and will emphasize your skills and experiences that the employer can use. Be sure to be positive, enthusiastic and honest.

Visualizing your success

For the longest time, I have dreamed of blocking a field goal in a crucial game. It is always the last play of the game in the playoffs and we are up by two points. I get off on the snap of the ball, low to the ground and charge over the guard in front of me. I see the ball out of the corner of my eye just as it gets to the hands of the holder. The kicker starts to make his downward motion to kick my team right out of the game. As he gets closer, so do I. The guard that I had tramped begins shouting, "NOOOOOO," simultaneously as I reach out. My body stretches out like a bridge over a great chasm with my hands out in front of me like a super hero through the stratosphere. I hear a loud thud of the ball being kicked. Then a fraction of a second later there is another. I catch the ball as it is being kicked. It hits my hands and rolls underneath me and I just lay there. The game is over. We win.

I have had the same types of dreams when it came to my writing and painting. I dreamed that my paintings would hang in a gallery and people would come from as far as Japan to see my work. Visualizing success is something that we all do as athletes. We see the circumstances play over and over again in our heads and we train ourselves to react. The same can be said for other occupations. Soldiers and police officers play out scenarios in training and in their heads so that they can react without hesitation when a problem presents itself. It is the same way on Wall Street, at the corporate offices of ESPN, Microsoft and hundreds upon hundreds of other companies. By creating a positive mental picture of yourself being successful in the career that you choose, it can help you overcome any obstacles that may present themselves.

Set long-term goals

In order to get to where you want to go, you have to map out a plan or agenda. Now is the right time to begin mapping out the career that's ahead of you. What is important to you, what do you enjoy or do not enjoy doing, what skills do you have to offer, what kind of work you are best qualified for and lastly, what are your future plans. How long do you want to stay in that particular occupation?

Regardless if you are a high school freshman or college freshman, it's not too early to start making the necessary contacts. Start today researching for that dream career. Go to the library, look on the Internet and/or call potential employers for information about the qualifications of certain positions in their company. Then figure out what classes you will have to take to make it a possibility for your to pursue. Also, ask about internships and summer jobs. Working on the job will give you a better perspective of the particular job and the commitment that it takes to be successful.

By participating and being proactive in your career development, you are able to enter the job market with more marketable skills than the average college graduate. In addition, your athletic background tells potential employers that you are a hard working, team-oriented individual who knows how to set goals and meet them.

What does the job require?

What does the job require? Knowledge, training, needed skills, duties and responsibilities, working conditions, e.g., hours, physical demands of the job, physical environment, salary range or compensation for work, opportunities for advancement, related occupations and future job outlook.

To be able to enter the job market with marketable skills, on-the-job-experience becomes very valuable! Summer jobs and internships can expose you to potential careers. It can also give you the work experience employers are looking for in new employees. The summer before I started high school I worked for a computer company, making scusis cables. It was actually a lot of fun. Every time I see one, it reminds me of taking the bus early in the morning to get to work by 7:30 a.m. Eating lunch from one of those mobile cafeterias. Then taking the bus home in the evening at 4:00 p.m. It was a lot of work, but it was a good experience.

By the time I got to college, I had enough work experience to be able to work during the summers as an intern and get credit for school at the same time.

A summer job can be full-time or part-time depending on the company and the time that you have to work. With hours ranging from 20 hours up to 40 per week for up to four months, the opportunity to work in a career enhancing occupation will help prepare you for the demands of your future employer. How to communicate with people, how to work in a team environment outside the locker room and how to work within the expectations of others in a real world setting is an important lesson.

Different and somewhat more beneficial than a summer job to a college student is an internship. An internship allows you the opportunity to combining academic credit and work experience in a field you are considering for your career. Usually unpaid, the experience itself is geared toward applying the academics of the classroom to the actual experience in your field of interest. A faculty professor in the department in which you apply for the internship, in association with your employer, will review your work with the cooperation of your employer to ensure that the appropriate academic credit can be given based on your performance.

The experience of working in your field of interest is an invaluable way of exploring your career possibilities and gaining work skills valued in the marketplace.

Check yourself

Create favorable results by researching and constantly evaluating your options and possible outcomes.

Chapter 6
Nutrition, diet and conditioning

Your body is your tool

Professional sports is like no other occupation because it requires aptitude in areas such as physics, mathematics, simple geometry, communications, chemistry and physical education. I know what you're thinking. How do math and chemistry figure into professional athletics? Well, believe it, they do. The physical education part is easy: how to stretch, improve running technique and conditioning. But science and communication skills are what each individual uses every day to perform on the practice field, in the meeting room and on game day. How do you think a golfer determines the speed of his swing as he approaches the pin? Answer: Math, because he knows the yardage between his lie and the flag's location.

What about physics? Let's go back to our golf example. When determining the club to use on the approach shot to the green, the golfer has other factors to consider. The wind. Is it blowing in your face? If it is, how hard? The green, is it down hill? Is the green fast or slow? All these variables have to be accounted for before the golfer strikes the ball.

In football, when tackling Jerome Bettis, what would be the best angle to take and how fast do you run in order to keep him from making a first down? You must use physics to get to that answer.

Jerome =	M3(Mass3)
Speed =	V(velocity)
Distance =	D (10 yards)
Force of Impact =	FI

M3 + V = FI
FI*D = Tackle for Loss/Fumble/Game Winning Play

At what speed would player B travel to stop Jerome from getting a first down?

What angle will you have to take?

Are you going to have help when you get there?

Did you eat the right foods before the game?

That last question may appear to be in the wrong place, but it's not. That's the thought process each player goes through before he makes a tackle and the right foods eaten before the game may determine your ability for split-second thinking.

Your brain is the number-one body tool you work with, so it must be kept in top working condition at all times. Make yourself better by thinking and making choices. Your mind gives your body direction and tells it what to do after you train it to perform. Outside athletics, in microseconds the brain tells the carpenter where to place the nail, then tells his hand to use the hammer to hit the nail on the head, not to hit his fingers. It tells the bus driver when to stop and start and it tells the artist what brush to use or the type of paint to place on the palette. Your body needs your mind to be able to function as efficiently as possible. How you treat it is important.

As an athlete, the biggest asset you have is your body. To increase your performance and get the desired results out of your body, you must maintain it through exercise and nutrition. How do you do that? One way to help improve your performance is through diet. No, not eating salads and having a crouton for dinner or even a meal replacement drink, but watching what you eat and knowing what you put into your body. We will talk about good foods and those which can maximize mental and physical performance.

Look at your hands. What do you need them for in your sport? Look at your legs. Would you be able to run without them? Of course not. Your fingers, your toes, your eyes – all these components make up your vehicle for success. Let's not forget your heart, lungs and the blood that runs through your body. All these movements and organs need fuel to work efficiently and productively. If you take care of your body with the proper nutrition and rest, it will reward you with peak performance. If you abuse it with foreign and sometimes fatal substances, you will not only hurt your body but possibly kill yourself. So it's important to have a great diet and eat the proper foods that allow you to live a healthy lifestyle and live happily.

The basics of nutrition

Nutrition is one important component of maximum physical development which most workout programs overlook. Establishing a foundation of good health and good eating habits early in life will help you maintain an active lifestyle and, most importantly, a healthy one. Every person needs the four basic nutrients: water, carbohydrates, protein and fat. Athletes need more of them because of the work they require from their bodies. Skipping meals to lose weight is counterproductive and will not allow for progress in the training program.

Although I am certainly not a doctor nor a nutritionist/dietitian, I can say that the ideal mixture of the basic nutrients for me has been the following: carbohydrates for approximately 50-60 percent of caloric intake; protein for approximately 20-25 percent of caloric intake; and fats for 15-20 percent of caloric intake. This is very important to remember because the four basic nutrients provide the body with its energy. In addition to the four basics, we also need vitamins and minerals to function daily. It has been estimated that there are approximately 50 nutrients in foods that are essential for the body's growth, maintenance and repair. These minerals are found in carbohydrates, fats and proteins.

Choosing the healthiest forms of these nutrients and eating them in the proper balance enables your body to function efficiently at a higher level of performance. Think again about the Jerome Bettis example. It all happens in a matter of split seconds.

Your library is well-stocked with books about nutrition and training. Pick one with a down-to-earth approach. I got pretty big and strong on my grandmother's cooking, so don't experiment with something exotic. Of course, the best advice is to check with your doctor. Doctors know the most about nutrition; they spend years just studying the body, and your family doctor knows your individual body best.

A word of caution. You'll meet people at the gym who claim to know everything about nutrition and training. They don't. They got their information from a buddy or from some questionable Internet site or from the back of a package. Get good information and don't settle for the tales of the gym guru.

Taking care of your body is critical for an athlete. Remember this: keep your food **simple, fresh** and **natural.** It's hard to go wrong if you stick to those rules. Fast food, by the way, is almost never simple. Fruits and vegetables are.

Water

Water is the mother of all nutrients. It is involved in every function of the body. It helps transport nutrients and waste products in and out of cells. It maintains the body's temperature and by drinking at least six to eight, 8-ounce glasses of water each day you can be assured your body has all it needs to maintain good health, according to *Elements of Nutrition, Diet and Wellness.* The average male is 60 percent water, the average female is 50 percent. But the obese person may be closer to 40 percent water. A muscular person, on the other hand, may be 70 percent water. Athletes who have a higher muscle mass and a low fat content have a relatively high body water content. In addition, the presence of high water content decreases the chances of muscular cramps due to dehydration. Caffeine and soft drinks also dehydrate you, causing increased urine production. So, remember to drink your water!

With the loss of water comes the loss of electrolytes, vitamins and minerals that can be replaced by consuming sports drinks during and following exercise. These drinks can enhance dehydration, but to insure against dehydration, consume plenty of fluids while exercising. You will perform best when your fluid intake is higher than your fluid loss.

Do: Drink plenty of water before, during and after exercise. Consume more than you lose. Keep a water bottle with you at all times.

Don't: Drink coffee, soft drinks or beverages high in caffeine or alcohol before, during or after exercising.

What are carbohydrates?

Carbohydrates, such as sugar and starch, are divided into two categories – simple carbohydrates and complex carbohydrates. Simple carbohydrates, sometimes called simple sugars, are represented by lactose (milk, sugar), sucrose (table sugar), fructose (fruit sugar) and sugar in other forms. Fruits are one of the richest sources of simple carbohydrates. Because they are mostly made up of water, the sugar and calorie content is relatively low and therefore healthier for you. On the other hand, refined simple carbohydrates such as table sugar and honey are good for quick energy, but crash you back down to earth after the effect has worn off. Cookies, soft drinks, and candy, as well as other snack foods, are usually loaded with these types of calories and will have the same effect if you depend on them for your main energy source. If consumed in large quantities over a long period of time, they can be quite unhealthy and lead to a number of disorders such as diabetes and hypoglycemia (low blood sugar). In addition, this type of unhealthy diet is full of calories that, if not used quickly, will be stored as fat. Here's one for you: FAT is the enemy of SPEED. Does that make sense?

Complex carbohydrates break down slower, meaning a constant source of energy is provided to help you sustain a steady pace for a longer period of time. Foods rich in complex carbohydrates are grains, pasta, potatoes and other vegetables. It is recommended that about 60 percent of your total daily caloric intake be made up of these kinds of carbohydrates to maintain a healthy diet. These foods are best when unrefined and fresh because they are full of nutrients, vitamins and a great source of fiber. A high fiber diet helps the body digest and move waste out of the intestine faster. It also reduces the risk of digestive anxiety, constipation and hemorrhoids.

To get the most out of your body, avoid simple sugars like candy, soft drinks and products made with table sugar. Eat plenty of complex carbohydrates to get the most out of your mind and body.

Do: Eat fresh fruits and vegetables, grains and pasta and drink plenty of water.

Don't: Consume large quantities of products made with refined sugar and soft drinks.

Proteins

Protein is essential in the development and growth of the body and repair of tissue. It provides energy and serves as the major source for the manufacturing of enzymes, hormones, growth and antibodies. The proteins in animal and plant foods are composed of structural units called amino acids. When protein is consumed, the body breaks it down into amino acids. Some amino acids are called nonessential, meaning they are not necessary, because the body cannot produce them itself.

Because of the importance of consuming proteins, they have been broken into two distinct categories, complete and incomplete proteins. Complete proteins contain an ample amount of all the essential amino acids. These proteins are found in meats, eggs, fish, poultry and cheese. Incomplete proteins contain only some of the essential amino acids and these proteins are found in fruits and leafy green vegetables. Although meat is the highest form of complete protein, it can be supplemented with a combination of other sources. Brown rice, corn, nuts or wheat combined with beans will provide the complete protein you need. Supplements such as protein powders and bars can also be a source of nutrients that your body needs to function efficiently, but don't depend solely on them for your main source of nutrition. (For more information, see Supplements)

Do: Eat a combination of foods high in good protein like chicken, fish, turkey, eggs, milk, brown rice, beans and corn, in conjunction with fruits and vegetables.

Don't: Supplement your protein intake with incomplete proteins and /or replacement meals. A salad and a protein shake are not enough.

Fats

Fats are the most concentrated source of food energy. One gram of fat supplies about nine calories. Fat is the body's only source of linoleic acid, a nutrient that is essential to growth, healthy skin and hair. As an athlete you will use carbohydrates and fats as sources of energy. Some athletes burn up to 75 percent of their energy from carbohydrates and 25 percent from fat during exercise mainly because carbohydrates are readily available. Fats take a little more time to break down. Carbohydrates are a good source of energy for short distance sprints and explosive movements. Workouts that are low impact and sustained for 12 to 30 minutes will burn more fat than carbohydrates in most athletes, so a proportioned, balanced diet is important.

Fats insulate and protect the body's organs from trauma and exposure to cold. Fat is also involved in the absorption and transportation of fat soluble vitamins. Fats are divided into two categories, saturated and unsaturated. As a rule, saturated fat is solid at room temperature and is derived mainly from animal sources (butter and lard) and unsaturated fat is liquid at room temperature and is found mainly in plant sources (olive oil, corn oil and canola). Some research suggest fats that are consumed from animal sources can be dangerous to the body because they raise the cholesterol level in the blood. That places more pressure on your heart and arteries. Unsaturated fat from corn, soybean and certain fish are healthier and help lower your cholesterol level. Both need to be in your diet but should make up only 10-15 percent of your total caloric intake.

Do: Eat foods that are low in fat (saturated and/or unsaturated).

Don't: Make your diet more than 15 percent saturated or polyunsaturated fat.

Vitamins

Why do we need vitamins? Vitamins are organic molecules or food substances the body cannot manufacture itself. Vitamins assist in converting food into energy.

Needed in relatively small amounts, vitamins are readily available in fresh green and yellow vegetables, fresh fruits, whole grains, fish, poultry and red meat. People who are active and exercise a lot should consider taking a multi-vitamin. Because of your activity, it is likely you lose a lot of vitamins and minerals in your perspiration.

Minerals contribute to how the body regulates itself. They combine with vitamins to form enzymes that are responsible for body regulating functions, such as blood clotting, muscles contracting and the regulation of a normal heart rhythm. Minerals like iron, calcium and phosphorus are used to carry the oxygen in your blood.

They also build bones and teeth. For peak performance, you need vitamins and minerals to function efficiently.

Do: Get your vitamins from a good source of fresh vegetables and foods that are high in them. Consider a multi-vitamin.

Don't: Forget the importance of minerals to the body's daily functions.

Fill your diet with fast foods like tacos and hamburgers, which are not efficient sources of vitamins and minerals and include a lot of fat. Remember, fat is the energy of speed.

Supplements

Multi-vitamins are considered supplements because they replace something your body needs or add something your body doesn't get enough of naturally. Supplements help athletes get stronger and faster, help increase energy level for optimum performance, aid in recovery after activity, and are good for general health. The harder you work, the more your body needs to recover. A protein bar or a protein shake after your workout is okay and recommended to help your body recover and provide some source of energy until your next meal. But supplements are not a replacement for eating a good, healthy balanced meal and not all supplements are recommended or even safe.

Most of the products sold for energy come loaded with caffeine or some other ingredient that promises a burst of energy. They perk you up and then you crash (kind of like our simple carbohydrates). They also have the tendency to dehydrate and cause cramping. You can't afford to risk injury because of an insufficient diet. Before you decide to buy something to put in your body just because it was endorsed by a Pro Bowler or an All-Star second baseman, ask your parents and/or coaches or check out the facts from a certified nutritionist. They should be able to tell you the effects of the supplement.

One of the hottest products on the market is creatine. Creatine is a compound that is made naturally in the body (primarily in the liver) which is used to supply energy to the muscle. It is composed of three amino acids: argentine, methionine and glycine, bound together chemically. Once manufactured in the liver, it is carried in the bloodstream, then transported into the muscle cells. Once inside the muscle cells, creatine is linked to a phosphate group and stored in the cell until used as energy. Quite simply, creatine monohydrate increases the amount of energy available to the muscle so that it can do more work and decrease the time of fatigue. Before using creatine or any other supplement, consult a doctor or certified nutritionist.

Do: Ask adults or other qualified individuals any questions about supplements.

Do: Know what you are putting in your body.

Don't: Be influenced by magazine ads and testimonials. Taking supplements can be expensive to your wallet and your life.

Don't: Put just anything in your body.

Gaining control of your diet takes you back to the big three: attitude, discipline and commitment. Athletes adopt an attitude of taking care of their bodies. Taking care requires discipline. When your body wants to stop for tacos at midnight, you must resist. Each time you resist the wrong foods, you show your commitment to excellence.

Weight Training

One of the most important determining factors to your success in athletics will be physical conditioning, which includes weight training. For a long time, people were concerned that lifting weights would make them stiff or muscle-bound and if children lifted weights it would stunt their growth. Did you know that the Green Bay Packers were one of the first football teams to lift weights in the 1960s to increase their strength and endurance? After the Packers won the first two Super Bowls, weight training became a regular routine of every team in the NFL. In basketball, players like Karl Malone and Grant Hill have programs that help keep them competitive on the court. In baseball, soccer, swimming, skiing, and even golf, weight programs help increase individual performance.

According to the latest research, weight training for adolescents is physically safe. Studies have been done which suggest the many ways lifting weights reduces the risk of injury. It increases the strength of bones due to the stress of weight lifting and adds on more bone-building materials, such as calcium, to increase bone density. Increased circulation, muscle and tendon strengthening, flexibility and increased self-esteem may also be benefits of a good workout program. If you decide to start a weight lifting program, it is important that you first consult an adult on proper technique and safety and you should absolutely consult your doctor before you begin. Start slowly and enjoy yourself.

A proper weight-training routine is important for a number of reasons:

1. **Health** – healthy heart, lungs, muscles and increased metabolism, increased lean body mass.

2. **Mental capacity** – focus, concentration, confidence and appearance.

3. **Competition** – build strength, endurance, agility and recovery time.

These variables are important to every person who has ever, or will ever, participate in athletics. Be sure to check with your coach or someone who is certified to train or supervise a program for you.

Many weight training programs are designed to train different parts of the body on different days. That way, the part you train Monday has Tuesday to recover. Many athletes divide workouts into those aimed at the legs and lower body and those aimed at arms and upper body. They throw in cardiovascular days, aimed at exercises to increase heart rate, like jogging or bicycling.

Weight training programs often alternate between free weights and machines. Each provide different benefits to the body. It's good to have a weight training partner who can spot you when using free weights and generally cheer you on while you cheer for them.

Again, weight training involves the big three: attitude, discipline and commitment. Weight training can actually improve your attitude by improving your confidence. It helps by allowing you to set small goals you can achieve with the discipline of working out every day, rain or shine. Your commitment will be evident in the way you stick to your plan.

Weight training allows you to see commitment in action. Today you bench press 135 pounds. Next week, after two more sessions at 135, you move up to 140. With weight training you can see your body and your mind building for excellence.

Warm-up

This is a key to a good workout that people often forget. Warm-up first. Imagine starting a car in the winter in the northern climates. You know that sound it makes, like it's trying too hard to get going. Well, that's what your body does when it's not warmed up correctly. It struggles to get going. The warm-up will increase a huge part of any good workout routine. In fact, it should be the first part of every workout program.

A routine of jumping rope or bike riding for five to ten minutes is important. This helps circulate blood and oxygen to your muscles and organs; it also helps loosen stiff joints. It gives your lungs and heart a chance to get moving at an up-tempo pace. Most importantly, a good warm-up routine prepares your body for the physical stress that will be applied to it. After your five-to-ten minute warm-up, a good stretch is essential to your weight-training routine.

Flexibility

Flexibility in a muscle group or joint area is an important aspect of conditioning. It allows freedom of movement. A tight muscle cannot react properly to stress or changes in speed. A relaxed muscle has increased circulation which benefits the removal of waste products that accumulate during exercise, as well as delivery of nutrients to the muscles. This increased blood supply will help with short and long-term muscle recovery. To ensure your muscles are warm, stretch before exercise.

After a wonderful eight-to-ten-minute bike ride, rope jumping session or whatever warm-up you choose, don't forget to stretch. A nice easy one will get you going in the right direction. Stretching helps prevent injuries by elongating the muscles and tendons attached to our bones. In a relaxed state, our muscles become shortened and tight. Stretching immediately promotes an increased blood flow to these muscles and tendons. This action increases their elasticity and contraction time, helping to make movements less dangerous to causing injury. Stretching also helps joints function in a larger range of motion, which is important when exercising different muscle groups. Don't rush; some people actually get hurt or injured while stretching. Remember, take your time. Don't bounce up and down; go slow and control each movement. Give yourself a good five minutes total, taking 30 seconds for each stretching exercise, to make the most of your workout.

Don't get in a hurry and neglect your stretches. Have you ever watched the players at a professional baseball game when the stands are just beginning to fill? You'll see them all over the grass in various stages of stretching. They are stretching to avoid injury. Injury will set back your weight training program. Injuries may be so defeating that you quit working out altogether.

A pro tip: Always take time to get loose first.

Cool down

Last, but not least: Don't forget to cool down after your workout. Cooling down keeps your muscle elongated and supple. Stretching before your workout provides an opportunity for you to focus on what you are about to do and cooling down gives a chance to reflect on what you have accomplished.

Your fitness routine or weight-training program has to be one that will allow you to maximize your ability and be productive.

Conditioning

All sports demand a certain level of endurance as it relates to physical conditioning. Training your body and mind to withstand certain physical challenges and achieve goals motivates most individuals. When conditioning, concentrate and relax. Work on running in straight lines and finish every repetition you start. Always work on your running proficiency, as this will help you pace yourself to be able to run farther and faster. Make sure that you always put forth your best effort.

Injury

If you have an injury be sure to get the right help. You can't perform if you are not available.

Chapter 7

You've got the body: now make the grade(s)

Academically ineligible

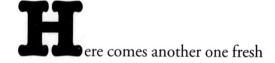ere comes another one fresh from the dictionary.

Opportunity is defined by *Webster's New World Dictionary* as follows:

1. *A combination of circumstances favorable for the purpose. 2. A good chance.*

One of the most disappointing moments in my high school career was receiving an F in science, which made me academically ineligible for football in the fall of my sophomore year. At the end of my freshman year, I thought I was the king of the hill because of my experience practicing on the varsity team. I also wrestled varsity a couple of times and I lettered in track. The success I had in athletics as a freshman gave me a slightly big head. I walked around campus with my jersey on long after the football season. Because of this newly found attention, I neglected my studies and paid dearly for it. I was crushed, but I deserved it.

My grandmother put it bluntly, "No good grades, no football." Period. From that day on, I promised myself I would never be academically ineligible again. Later, I would be one credit shy of graduating from high school. What was I going to do? I had no clue. I had to see a school counselor to find out how to make up what I failed to do earlier. He said I had to attend night school to make it up. It was impossible for me to make up the class in high school because all my electives were taken up with sports, so night school was the only solution.

That solution was also a problem. I was always playing a sport after school. So, I was confronted with a tough choice, was it going to be sports or night school? One had to be sacrificed or I would have been forced to take a class during the summer, which meant I couldn't go to a summer football camp at one of the local colleges. Instead of missing the football camps during the summer, I decided to sacrifice wrestling my junior year because football had become the most important sport to me. I waited until my junior year to sign up for the course and had to really work to keep up with the schedule. I couldn't miss a class or everything would have been messed up. Any chance of a scholarship and graduating with my class was dependent on me completing one class.

Night School

Looking back on the experience, it wasn't as bad as I thought. In fact, it was my first college campus experience. It gave me a preview of what I was going to see one day. Between the time I received my first and only F in high school and when I attended the football camp at Berkeley, I had become one of the most recognized athletes in the Bay Area. This was when I was being scouted by several colleges for what eventually became a football scholarship. Schools like Washington, Washington State, UCLA, Oklahoma, San Jose State, Oregon and Oregon State University were sending letters and publications about their programs to my aunt's and uncle's house and to the school. My coaches told me they were getting phone calls every week about the recruiters who were interested in me. The questions I weighed were: What school would I choose? What would I study? What would I become? Did I want to stay home or did I want to travel far away? As I thought about the answers to those questions, I started becoming more and more interested in professional football because college football was closer than I ever anticipated.

I had to take care of this night class first. It was held at the junior college and started after my junior year football season. School was growing more important than ever and grades became even more important to securing my future. Not only did I have to pass a class in night school, I had to study for college entrance exams and pass the SAT or the ACT by March so I could take it again before my senior year, if necessary. So the pressure was on and I could feel it. After school, my grandmother picked me up and then dropped me off at the college, or my friends Mike and Eric dropped me there. I had class every Tuesday and Thursday night for 90 minutes. After class, I did my homework while waiting for someone to pick me up. Once I figured out I could use that idle time to do my homework or something else productive, instead of just waiting, I got a lot done and was ahead of the game.

Great Study Habits Will Help You to Be Successful

Every fall, every winter and spring, playbook after playbook is given out to hundreds of college freshmen wanting to become professional athletes in every imaginable sport.

In each group one person thinks he or she is the greatest athlete ever to come down the pike, so the playbook is ignored. That person may have been the best athlete in little league, the best in Pop Warner football, the best athlete in high school, but now they are just another individual trying to get a job. At this time, mediocre study habits and terrible time management skills begin to catch up to our aspiring professional. Because that person never learned how to prepare for this level of success, a lesson is learned the hard way. They get cut. And, *if* they come back, it will be with better preparation - better study habits.

One of the basic fundamental elements of success in any endeavor is a level of competence in the subject matter being pursued. One way to absorb information is to be able to look at a subject and break it down into components you can understand. Even in the volatile world of athletics an activity as simple as studying for an extra hour becomes pivotal. The margin between one athlete and another is so small, the advantage will go to the individual who studied that extra hour before bed or took the time to shoot those 100 free throws. This is a perfect example of the commitment we've been talking about in action.

There are bus stations and airports full of these great athletes at the end of the fall, winter and spring trying to figure out what went wrong.

Instilling a Positive Work Ethic and Study Habits

How many times have you shrugged off responsibilities until another time because you would rather do something else, or you didn't try as hard when the coach wasn't looking? You aren't the only one who has done that. Even as professional athletes we have, at one point, neglected a responsibility or two and even relaxed when the coach stopped looking. The problem arrives when this behavior becomes acceptable to us.

Each of us is responsible for certain things. As young aspiring athletes, you are responsible for training your minds and bodies for the challenges of competition. You are responsible for finding out what your physical and mental boundaries are and pushing yourself beyond them.

The use of discipline comes in how you prepare for the game, how you practice and how you approach the challenge before you. How many times has your coach given you instructions to study your playbook? Or, how many times has your mother told you to take the trash out. At that point, you can make one of two decisions: Study, take the trash out or not study, not take the trash out. A person who has good discipline will do both now. No matter what the task might be.

One day, your ability to be disciplined in study habits, follow instructions and/or get a job done in a timely fashion, will give you the opportunity to shine you have been looking for.

Here are some study tips that helped me in my quest for success.

1. Be prepared. Have the appropriate materials (i.e., pencil or pen and a notebook) ready when you attend class or team meetings.

2. Take legible notes on the key points of the lecture. Rewrite and review these notes right after class.

3. Don't be afraid to ask questions. There are no stupid questions. Remember: it is your future at stake.

4. Don't procrastinate. If it needs to be done, do it now. Don't wait for someone to tell you.

5. Get organized! Keep a calendar in your book bag/backpack. Write down important due dates for assignments and appointments.

6. Always do the best you can do. Anything less than your best is unacceptable.

7. Always be prepared to rise to any challenge.

Without the discipline to learn, being a successful athlete, or any type of professional, is almost impossible.

Every Opportunity is an Excellent Teaching Tool

Sometimes, all we need is a good chance, or a favorable circumstance, to achieve our goals. These "good chances" or "favorable circumstances" are better known as opportunities. Each of us is presented with opportunities every day. We just need to be ready to recognize them for what they are, chances.

How many times have you heard the story of a great high school athlete who has every college in the country after them, but, that same athlete is unable to see the scholarship offers as a chance for an education? Occasionally overlooked is the fact that they must first be admitted scholastically to the university. Quite often, an inadequate GPA prevents that.

Another familiar story is a star college athlete, with a good chance at being drafted, who drops out of school with three months left in the semester. That athlete did not take advantage of his chance to finish his or her college education. Not only are those bad decisions, they are lost opportunities.

The chance to go to college on scholarship is an honor. The opportunity to earn a degree, while participating in something you love, is special. If I hadn't gone to college, I don't think I would have been able to dream about traveling to different countries around the world. College opened my eyes and my mind to something bigger than San Jose.

You could say going to college opened a gateway for me. That gateway wasn't to the NFL; that gateway was to the world in which we live. Because I took advantage of the education provided me, I was able to function outside of athletics.

College athletes who drop out because they think the NFL draft is a winning lottery ticket are in for a big surprise. From where I sit, the NFL doesn't want you to come out of college unprepared.

If you have bad study skills or you have questionable discipline, don't expect things to immediately click in the NFL scene. Bad habits carry over into NFL meetings and on the field. Then the NFL stands for "Not For Long." The best thing you can do to insure your future is graduate. Graduation gives you the opportunity to establish yourself in another field during your career as a professional athlete. I suggest taking some business courses. The more business knowledge you have, the better off you'll be because professional athletics is a business.

Here are some tips that helped me in my quest for success. They may also help you:

1. Be prepared. An opportunity might just be waiting around the corner. Your challenge is to find out whether or not it is a good one. Look at the lesson I learned from going to the Eagles camp not fully prepared. In my first Chiefs training camp, my preparations didn't pay immediate dividends. But the Chiefs must have seen something they liked. They had me back - and I made the team.

2. Evaluate the outcome in your mind. If it's good, take advantage of it. If it's bad, take note and walk away. I am not a quitter, yet I had to stand up and walk away from a situation I knew I had no chance of winning when I asked for my release

from the Eagles. You can always ask for help if you need to make a crucial decision.

3. Don't be afraid to ask questions. Remember, it's your future at stake.

4. Create your own opportunities: Research, Revise, Review and Respond.

Always be prepared to rise to any challenge.

Education

Making the choice to go to college is a big step in any young adult's life. Talk about peer pressure. The decision to pursue higher education is one that has to be planned and approached with a certain degree of responsibility. In your group of peers, some decide to pursue the opportunity to attend college, others make the decision to stay behind and do nothing. They would rather work enough to get by as opposed to securing their own future. Going to college is more than the chance to play college sports or pursue professional athletics.

So why go to college? Why do most kids who aren't athletes go to college? To get an advanced degree for a great occupation. If you surround yourself with quality individuals who have aspirations of going to college, then, believe me, it will soon rub off on you. You can bet on it. Did you know hundreds of colleges are looking to give scholarships away to deserving students and student-athletes like you? Seriously.

They need you to make their schools more competitive in athletics and you have a special gift to use in exchange for room, board and tuition. Where do you want to go? Don't be the one left behind. Pursue your dreams. Outside of your chance of playing college athletics and being successful enough to move on to a professional career in sports, the pursuit of a college education is the most important thing you will ever do. I'll mention it until it's ingrained: The odds are 10,000 to one against you making it in the arena of professional athletics. You will be one of thousands believing you have a chance to play professionally and, in every case, the advantage goes to the one who is prepared for his or her future outside of athletics. The opportunity to create the future of your choice is yours and that's what college is all about. Choice.

Having a college degree creates a distinct advantage for you. Did you know that the average income for a person without a high school diploma is $14,000 a year? After taxes, that gives you less than a $1,000 a month to live on. That may sound good to some of you, but that's living from paycheck to paycheck. There's no security in not knowing if you will be able to eat tomorrow, never having the opportunity to move forward and secure a future for yourself or make any plans to have a family. What does a person offer an employer if he can't even finish high school? Believe me, very little. You must understand there is more and, if you want it, you're going to have to work for it. Once you understand that, you can begin to take the necessary steps to pursue your college education.

Graduate from high school and decide to pursue higher education

The average salary for a high school graduate is $20,000, so your diploma is essentially worth $6,000 a year (Remember the $14,000 a year salary without the diploma?). The average salary for a college graduate with a bachelor's degree is $35,000. That's $15,000 every year of your life for completing four more years of school. The average salary of someone with a graduate degree is $55,000, and with a doctorate, the average is $75,000. The lack of a high school education hardly gives a person with the necessary means to provide for himself. A person with only a high school education today will have a hard time making ends meet.

Trust me, a Kobe Bryant or a Kevin Garnett (both young NBA players) comes along once in a blue moon. You probably never heard of Bill Willoughby, have you? He jumped from high school to the NBA in 1975, the first non-center to do so. After six seasons in the NBA, Willoughby averaged 6.0 points a game and 3.9 rebounds a game. That's probably why you never heard of him. By age 26, he was out of the NBA. In 1995, after realizing the void in his life left without a college education, Willoughby enrolled at Fairleigh Dickinson University in Teaneck, New Jersey. He was 38 years old when he went back to college.

To his credit, Willoughby didn't feel it was too late to seek his college education. Make your opportunity to pursue college a priority, alongside excelling at sports. Be a true example of a *student*-athlete.

Seek the advice of your high school (and college) academic advisor(s)

Most advisors have about 100 students they hope to direct to the right path. To find out if you are on the right path academically, you need to schedule a meeting with your advisor at least once a quarter. This will enable you to make sure your test scores are high enough and you are meeting the curriculum standards most colleges want. Your high school advisor will be able to tell you what you need to know to be admitted into the school of your choice, i.e., the required grade point average (GPA), courses of study, evaluation letters, etc. Your advisor will be able to tell you when and where the entrance exam testing will be taking place, explain how to raise your GPA or make up lost credits because of a class deficiency (I found out that drill, as you know), detail the proper way to complete a college application and prepare for the interviews.

It also helps that your parents know your academic goals so they can be supportive. If you're in a family situation without the attention needed from your parents, it is imperative for you to stay on top of things with the help of your advisor. If your parents are closely monitoring your progress, they may have some tips that your advisor doesn't know or maybe forgot. Regardless, if you are fortunate enough to receive a scholarship, your parents, or whoever is acting as your guardian, need to be involved in your decision-making because, Lord willing, they will be your source of support emotionally and financially when you need them.

Typically, the role of academic advisors includes, but is not limited to, the following:

1. Assisting student-athletes in making informed decisions about choice of major and career.

2. Providing student-athletes the opportunity to explore career information resources.

3. Exploring experiential opportunities like internships, cooperative education, summer jobs, volunteer work.

4. Preparing student-athletes for life after college - mentally, physically, possibly spiritually. They should talk to you about adjusting to professional life.

5. Assisting students through the career-decision making process.

6. Alleviating stress caused by career uncertainty.

As naive college freshmen zone in on their first semester, predominantly thinking about their plan for professional sports, few really know the academic steps. Occasionally, even those who think they know, really don't. That's the reality. You could minimize the difficulty by using your academic advisors in the manner just described.

The first area of study most students have is in liberal arts, the study of everything. I was a liberal arts person because I wanted to know about everything. I started thinking about what I wanted to do outside of football. I thought about what I loved and what I enjoyed outside of athletics. I loved to paint and draw.

As I briefly mentioned, when I was being recruited as a high school senior, I took an interest in architecture. I thought the architecture department at Cal, as I found out during my recruiting visit there, was wonderful. An art degree was also a possibility for me or maybe architecture and art. I felt I could do and be anything. The next step was putting together a plan. I mapped out exactly what I needed to do to make it come true.

After thinking about all the possibilities, I called my academic advisor and scheduled a meeting to talk about what I wanted to do with my time at OSU. We met after I injured my knee in my freshman year and I told him what happened. The cast on my leg made it obvious. We discussed the possibilities and he even suggested thinking ahead to graduate school. I told him I wanted to be an artist or an architect, or both if possible. After talking to him, my eyes opened. I never thought about the possibilities of where I could go in life. I saw that anything was possible.

After the long conversation, we wrote out a plan. We listed the classes I needed over the four years, from general education to classes that pertained directly to an art major. With that plan in hand, the next step was applying it to the rest of my life and making sure it got done. The classes I had as a freshman in the winter of 1986 were mostly general education. Following the meeting, I had a new idea of the situation, so I had to concentrate on getting a routine that kept me focused on graduating.

My football season was over prematurely and I dealt with the possibility of not being able to play professional football, or not even getting another chance to play in college. I kept pretty much the same schedule with my classes and used the practice block for rehabbing my knee. Because of the injury, my life was changed. I began to approach every day with a purpose, as if my life depended on it. I didn't want to go back home; I wanted to graduate from college and go on to be a success in the world. I wasn't going to let the knee injury, or the pain of rehabilitation, deny me.

Keep this in mind if you get hurt playing sports in high school: with today's medical technology, plenty of high school athletes rebound strongly from injuries and successfully compete in college on athletic scholarships. Don't let the injury sidetrack you from your ultimate goal. Chances are, someone on your favorite professional team likely experienced a high school or college injury at one time or another. Though you may not be able to physically perform on the playing field, don't let it affect your performance in the classroom.

If you're not 100 percent sure of your career path following athletics, don't be intimidated by the prospects of changing your major when you reach college. I found out the hard way.

I learned my scholarship didn't pay for all the necessities like paint, canvas, paint brushes and clay for my art classes past basic drawing. So oil painting, sculpture or any other class that required me to purchase materials was out. I couldn't afford to pay for supplies out of my pocket, so I had to change majors.

I was hurt that I couldn't pursue art, but I had to continue my plan and I wasn't going to let a minor change hold me back. After soul-searching, I thought about what went on at home, recalling the randomness of crime I saw first-hand and knowing the violence that tore through the urban community. I decided the law as a career wasn't a bad idea. I thought about the difference I could make as a lawyer or a judge. Plus, I saw Blair Underwood play a lawyer on television and it seemed within reach. There weren't too many black lawyers I knew growing up in San Jose, so seeing Underwood's character portrayed on the TV series *L.A. Law* inspired me. I just decided I wanted to help in some way. I was once again off to my advisor to set my classes straight. Majoring in political science was the first step to making law a reality, so I tweaked my plan just a little bit with the idea of becoming a lawyer some day.

Take entrance exams

There are two types of entrance exams: the Standard Achievement Test (SAT) and American College Test (ACT). These tests are given four times a year and take no less than six hours to complete. Each of these tests consists of several parts that evaluate your reading, math, science and English comprehension. Your test scores alone will not determine your fate. The grades you received and the types of classes you took after your freshman year are big factors in the admissions evaluation process. A student with a high GPA and an average test score is just as competitive as a candidate with an average GPA and high test score. Other factors admissions officers evaluate are the application, letters of recommendation, leadership ability, awards, work experience and extracurricular activities. Admission officers realize students who are well-rounded in their activities will be great candidates to graduate from their university. Once they decide you are a match, the real work begins.

But remember this about the ACT and SAT. You can improve your scores by study. The library in your high school is the best place to look for material on how to enhance your test scores.

Design a personal and professional career plan

It takes a special kind of person to be a student-athlete, to be able to endure the constant demand for performance on and off the field. The commitment of being an athlete requires involvement in lifting, running, practice and participating in team-organized events. The challenges of the classroom environment require concentration, participation in classroom activities and study. Both activities require you to compete daily with student-athletes and non-athletes for a great performance. Whether it is on the basketball court or in Propaganda 201, the life of the student-athlete is always mentally challenging. Very few can handle the demands. Many student-athletes can't handle the pressure of doing both and either drop out of school completely or become a regular student.

I'll hammer away at the 10,000 to one odds of making it as a professional athlete. Your focus and dedication as a student-athlete are important to your success, not only during your college years, but in your professional career as well. Whether you make it as a pro or not, focus and dedication are keys.

The form which follows can help you to focus on goals. It provides an outline for you to follow so you can chart progress towards your long-term goals.

Long-term academic goal-setting

Write one goal that can be met within the school year.

1. Goal: _____

2. What could keep me from reaching this goal?

_____I don't really have the skills or knowledge needed.

_____I don't want it bad enough to work for it.

_____I'm afraid I might fail.

_____I'm afraid of what others might think.

_____Others don't want me to reach my goal.

_____The goal is really too hard to reach.

Other reasons might be: _____

Think about the specific steps you must take to reach your goal. Write them down and follow them.

Step 5. _____

Step 4. _____

Step 3. _____

Step 2. _____

Step 1. _____

Chapter 8

Leadership, peer pressure, do's and don'ts

Looking For Tomorrow's Leaders!

To lead is defined by *Webster's New World Dictionary* as follows:

1. *To direct, as by going before or along with.* 2. *To direct by influence.* 3. *To be head of.*

A leader is defined as

1. *One who leads.* 2. *A guiding head.*

In today's world, an ever-shrinking world crowded with billions and billions of us, we need leaders who will dare us to dream. Leaders are people who ask questions, people who do what needs to be done to make a positive difference in the lives of others, people who attract similar personalities and people who motivate. Most importantly, leaders do what it takes. When the coach is trying to teach a play, do you pay attention to detail? Or do you goof off in the back of the room and disrupt the meeting? When you don't understand a certain adjustment, do you ask the question? If someone else doesn't understand, even if they play the same position as you, do you volunteer to help them?

You see, it doesn't take a leader to identify the misfortunes of others, but it does take one to risk his or her own comfort to help improve the opportunities and lives of others. Leaders must identify unfavorable situations and improve them for the betterment of all without bias. That's what a leader must do. To lead is to have vision. When the coach demands extra laps to get in shape, do you step up to the front of the pack and lead your peers? Or do you sit in the middle and complain? A leader knows there is a purpose to his perspiration. If the nearest competitor to your position doesn't understand, do you help him or laugh at his ignorance? A leader reaches out to those in need because he knows that, down the road, that individual may have the opportunity to help the team. If he doesn't know how to perform correctly, the team will suffer.

As you read on, you will find that leadership and peer pressure, in many cases, go hand-in-hand. I found that out in college when I decided to join a fraternity. Not just any fraternity. I elected to pledge the greatest black fraternity in the world, Kappa Alpha Psi Fraternity, Inc. Everyone at one time or another in life wants to be in a group because of the status it commands. I wanted to belong. I needed to feel I was part of something special, something worthy of commitment and great substance. I saw other fraternities on campus and wasn't interested in belonging to a group where I was the only African-American. With the campus population of black students at less than one percent of the entire student body, I guess it shouldn't be a surprise I chose Kappa Alpha Psi.

Why do people join fraternities, you might ask? Well, for a number of reasons. You could say it's 1) for the parties and the girls, 2) the nice big house they live in or, 3) belonging to a group of people with similar goals and objectives. At OSU, Kappa Alpha Psi didn't have a house. If any parties were thrown, I laid low. No, I didn't join Kappa Alpha Psi for the parties or the entertainment factor. I joined for my future. That organization taught me more about being responsible for my own future and the importance of setting and working towards goals within a group of people who had similar aspirations, than anything else I've done.

Some of my leadership qualities must have come out while I was there because I was elected president of the fraternity my junior and senior years. I tried to carry those same qualities to the football field during my junior season at OSU. Against Cal, the school that no longer wanted to offer me a scholarship after my senior season in high school, I played well enough to earn my first Pac-10 Player of the Week honor. I forced a fumble – we won the game!

The next week we traveled to Boulder, Colorado, to play against the Buffaloes and I was the talk of the town. I remember as I was climbing on the bus after the game (which we lost, unfortunately), one of their offensive linemen looked like he was talking to his parents and commented on how they had to double-team me because I was quick and one of OSU's best players.

I took it to heart and tried to become even more of a leader. The next couple of weeks ahead of us were going to be tough…Fresno State at home, UCLA in Pasadena and Stanford in Palo Alto. We had to come together and play if we wanted to live up to our expectation of a winning season. We beat Fresno State, 21 -10, and I had two sacks. We stayed with UCLA the entire game, but lost 38-21.

I had three big hits on Troy Aikman that caused two fumbles. At Stanford, last-minute heroics led to a tie, 20-20.

After the 1988 season, I felt I was close to reaching the NFL and I didn't want to let go of the momentum. Before anything got in the way, I decided to stay the final summer, take a heavy class load and repeat the same routine that helped me in my junior year. By taking classes during the summer, I'd be in a position to graduate on time without a problem. I could feel all the anticipation building and I wanted it to happen. *I advise you to take charge of your own planning so that you can meet whatever obstacles are thrown your way.* There will be times when you need to take it upon yourself to make leadership decisions. That shows what my teammates thought about my leadership skills and the quality of choices I made.

In my senior season at college, I was elected one of the team captains.

From speaking in public representing my fraternity, I developed a feel for people. I also gained confidence speaking to people. I was comfortable with all I accomplished in such a short period of time at OSU and, after being president of my fraternity and captain of the football team, people knew who I was. The development of my leadership skills and my ability to be a self-starter was enough to impress Procter & Gamble to want to interview me, not just once, but three times. Then they offered me a job. I was in total shock. Procter & Gamble was recruiting *me*. The Communications/ Political Science/Art major was in demand. My Plan B was in place. Obviously, I felt good about it.

What does it take to be a leader?

It is said that leaders are like eagles. They never flock nor gather, they are found one at a time. Being one is a great responsibility and not easily maintained. People depend on you to provide an example they can follow without exception. They look to you for strength, confidence and motivation. A leader is at the disposal of the people he or she serves without exception.

Being the captain of the football, volleyball, baseball or basketball team is an honor and a privilege. What it says to the rest of the world, or team, is that you are trusted and respected by your peers to be the best representation of what they would like to be. You exemplify the group and the vision they see for themselves.

Here are some distinct qualities of leadership:

1. A moral foundation

2. Family and peer respect

3. Willingness to take responsibility

4. Capacity to catch or create a vision

It is not easy being a leader, but for those of you who are chosen, the reward is something you will always have, no matter what.

Here are some ways to help you know your leadership talents:

1. Know your strengths. What are you exceptional at?

What experiences do you bring to the table?

2. Get organized! Keep a calendar in your book bag /backpack. No one wants a leader who can't keep track of time.

3. Always do the best you can do. You are the model for the group.

4. Be enthusiastic! Always be positive and prepared to rise to any challenge.

Peer pressure

Some of the hardest decision-making you'll face will come at the expense of your closest friends. The decisions will be life-lasting because once you expose yourself to the options of right and wrong, positively and negatively, you must weigh the consequences of your actions. Your foundation of a positive attitude and discipline will help, but ultimately it will come down to you making a choice based on what you want for your life.

What can you do and say to stand up to peer pressure and still keep the friendships that are important to you? These skills are important because if you make the wrong decision, it can prevent you from living your dream and, instead, you will probably face unfavorable circumstances. On the other hand, if you make the right decision, not only will you be even more confident and able to withstand the pressure, you may convince others to do what's right. It's up to you.

There is a lot in the world today that has the appearance of a young adult telling you what is good for you. Television, magazines, newspapers and music all influence some of the decisions in your life. Media affects all of us. It is inevitable. It is inescapable. It's easy for someone like me to tell you not to listen and it's harder for you because there are a lot of pressures involved. The biggest influence on you are your friends and you have to be comfortable with yourself and them to be able to make the correct decision. Make a decision that will not jeopardize your future as a student-athlete. One that will not cause injury to yourself or anyone else. Ask yourself this question: What is a friend?

What is a friend?

To answer some of these questions about yourself and your friends, a couple of exercises in this chapter will help. The first section is about becoming a friend to yourself. The second section is about the best way to make and keep friends and the third section is about recognizing and redirecting peer pressure.

Be sure to read and fill out each question. If you have any questions, I'm sure one of your parents or an adult will be glad to help you.

What is a friend?

Is a friend someone who would allow you to hurt yourself or others?

Is a friend someone who would allow you to hurt yourself physically?

Is a friend someone who you can depend on to lift you up when you are feeling down?

Are you a good friend to yourself, do you treat yourself when you do well? Do you correct yourself when you do something wrong?

Friendship is one of the most important things in the lives of people your age. You may be asking yourself the following:

Do I have any real friends?

Can I trust my friends with my secrets?

Will they still want me for a friend if I do something stupid or different from them?

Will they force me to do things I really don't want to do?

Would they like me if they really knew me?

To have a friend, you have to be a friend. It's a two-way street. All of us at some point need someone to confide in, to be with, to help us get through a choppy stretch in our lives.

Be there for someone else when they need you. And, very likely, that person will be there for you when you need help.

Making Choices

Finding ways to help young people stand up to peer pressure is hard today because the pressure pulls from all directions. On television, music videos degrade women and endorse the use of violence as a means of solving problems. Prime time shows that do the same and use language and sexuality to get attention, and, of course, ratings.

Do I even need to say the word? Drugs. Drugs are everywhere. Drugs are always available. Right?

How many songs propose getting high to solve your problems? Unfortunately, a lot of today's popular songs fall into that category. Thing is, if you follow that advice the problem still exists, but now it is worse than before. You don't need drugs or alcohol to have a good time. If your car were low on gas, would you put sand in your gas tank?

The following exercises will help you recognize pressure situations and offer insight on how to respond. Read and answer every question. If you have any questions, ask an adult to help you.

Making and keeping friends

Here are three keys to making and keeping friends:

1. Be a good listener. Encourage the other person to talk about himself/herself.

2. Show the other person you are interested in him or her.

3. Make the other person feel special and important.

Key #1: Be a good listener.

Think of your last conversation with a friend. Who talked the most?

_____

What can you do to get the other person to talk about himself/herself?

_____

List some questions you could ask.

_____

_____

_____

Key #2: Show the other person you are interested in him or her.

Think of a person you are friends with or would like to be friends with.

Think about this person's family and friends, where he or she lives, where he or she goes to school, what special talents this person has and what his or her hobbies are. List the things about this person that you can show an interest in.

Key #3: Make the other person feel special or important.

Think again about your friend or the person you would like to befriend. Think about how this person looks, acts, thinks and feels. How could you make this person feel special?

What could you say?

_____

_____

What could you do?

_____

_____

In addition to the friend you've already thought about, think about one more friend or another person with whom you would like to be friends. Think about how this person treats other people and how he or she helps them. Could you make this person feel important?

What could you say?

_____

_____

What could you do?

_____

_____

Bad Stuff

In the pages following to the end of this chapter, I talk about steroids, drugs, alcohol and tobacco. I talk about ways in which these substances are harmful, and in some cases and for some age groups, are illegal. The National Clearinghouse for Alcohol and Drug Information is the reference source for the factual material.

Steroids

Growing up in the Bay Area of northern California, we had a lot of sports teams to follow, from the San Francisco '49ers and Giants to the Golden State Warriors and Oakland A's. Of all the teams that were visible, there was only one team for me. The Oakland Raiders. I loved the Raiders when I was a kid, probably because they were nasty and relentless, but primarily because of a guy named Lyle Alzado. He was this big, muscle-bound man with a beard and a scowl on his face that looked like it would intimidate the devil himself. He seemed to be afraid of nothing and no one. People moved out of his way. Other players were intimidated by his play. He was mean and I wanted to be like him.

As you know, I chose his number when I played high school football. I wanted to emulate his presence to everyone around me, especially on the football field. Wearing the number 77 became my signature; it meant I had a tradition to uphold. I had to be relentless and tough whenever I wore the number. I have always taken pride in my work ethic and the way I played the game. I play with a purpose all the time, relentless and tough. In 1991, I had the chance to finally meet number 77. I felt like an eight-year-old looking up to a favorite uncle or teacher. My words tripped out of my mouth and I stumbled to pick them up. He was real and I was in the same room with him and all I could do was smile and walk away.

Two years later, in 1993, my childhood hero died of complications due to his use of anabolic steroids. To me Lyle Alzado was as big as Superman or the Hulk. I mean, he could do anything. Right? I remember crying when I saw him being interviewed on television about his illness. He didn't look the same. He wasn't the same man I had seen as a warrior. The once towering man now looked withered and beaten. His life was slowly and painfully being taken. All because of a choice he made to take steroids at a time when doing so was the norm.

Because of Lyle Alzado, I was able to gain confidence and I still wear the number 77 for that reason. The number I wore as a college and high school football player means more to me now than ever. Now, I wear it as a memorial to the man who inspired my play. I learned one message from seeing him in such a terrible time in his life and listening to him, *anabolic steroids are not worth the risk.* Short-term gain is not worth losing a lifetime of experiences. Putting things in our bodies that we know so little about can, and will, hurt us.

With Alzado's death and the talk generated about the use of steroids by athletes in professional and amateur sports, the public was exposed to an ugly side of sports that had gone unseen and ignored for a long time. Yet, because of the attention and the publicity, more high school student-athletes began using steroids.

These athletes were looking for quick results in their workouts or a way to change their bodies, not really knowing what they were doing. According to a recent survey, the perception of the harmfulness of steroid use has decreased among both 12th graders and 8th graders. This fact is particularly disturbing because a person's usage of any substance is highly dependent on his or her understanding of how harmful it is. And if they had listened to the story of Lyle Alzado more closely, they would have known exactly how destructive steroids are.

Anabolic (building) androgenic (masculinizing) steroids, commonly known just as steroids, include the male hormone testosterone and its artificial derivatives. Steroids are used as treatment for certain diseases and testosterone deficiency. They are considered drugs and some are illegal. Since the late 1950s, steroids have gained popularity due to their use by professional athletes and non-athletes to improve their athletic ability and to look better.

Steroids do more than pump you up; they also destroy your body. They cause different parts of the anatomy to either shrink or swell depending on whether the user is male or female. Surprisingly, women use steroids too.

Many professional athletes have ruined their careers and lives by using steroids. Do you want to make the same mistake?

Major side effects
of steroids include:

- Liver tumors

- Jaundice

- Fluid retention

- High blood pressure

- Severe acne

- Yellowing of skin and eyes

- Trembling

- Weakening of tendons which may result in tearing or rupture

Physical side effects include:

In Males

- Testicles may become sterile

- Abnormal breast development

- Stunted growth

- Premature balding

- Severe acne

- Elevated cholesterol levels

- Elevated blood pressure

In Females

- Increased body hair
- A deeper voice
- Smaller breasts
- Fewer menstrual cycles
- Stunted growth
- Severe acne
- Elevated blood pressure
- Elevated cholesterol levels

Marijuana

Marijuana is the most widely used illicit drug in the United States and tends to be the first illegal drug used by teens. However, that is not to say the majority of teens use marijuana. In fact, according to a 1994 survey of high school seniors, while 30.7 percent had used marijuana sometime within the past year, 69.3 percent did not. Additionally, most marijuana users do not go on to use other illegal drugs.

Why do young people smoke pot? Some want to be "in," to look "cool." Others who are shy in social situations turn to it to loosen up and frequently make fools of themselves by doing things they later regret.

So, You Want to be a Pro?

To any and all who would be tempted by marijuana, I list below negative physical and mental effects of this drug.

Short-term effects of using marijuana include:

- Sleepiness and increased hunger
- Difficulty keeping track of time, impaired or reduced short-term memory
- Reduced ability to perform tasks requiring concentration and coordination, such as driving a car
- Increased heart rate
- Potential cardiac dangers for those with preexisting heart disease
- Bloodshot eyes
- Decreased social inhibitions
- Risk of paranoia, hallucinations and intense anxiety

Long-term effects of using marijuana include:

- Increased risk of chronic pulmonary disorders, including cancer
- Decrease in testosterone levels for men
- Increase in testosterone levels for women
- Lower sperm counts and difficulty having children in men
- Increased risk of infertility in women
- Psychological dependence requiring more of the drug to get the same effect

A recent study of 1,023 trauma patients admitted to a shock trauma unit (receiving only the most seriously injured accident victims), found that one-third had detectable levels of marijuana in their blood.

Some people find that marijuana can increase their appetites, which may lead to gorging on junk food and possible weight gain. If you, or someone you know, has been using marijuana, help is available. Talk to a school counselor, a friend or a parent.

Ten Reasons Not to Use Marijuana:

1. It's against the law.
Marijuana is an illegal substance. Depending on where you are caught, you could face a heavy-duty fine and jail time.

2. It clouds your judgment.
You do not function normally or concentrate normally under the influence of marijuana. It does not make you superhuman or free your mind.

3. You risk infertility.
Marijuana has been shown to lower sperm counts in men and increase the risk of infertility in women.

4. Using drugs increases the risk of injury.
Car crashes, falls, burns, drowning and suicide are all linked to drug use.

5. You can't keep your edge.
Drugs can ruin your looks, make you depressed, and contribute to situations that compromise your ability to learn.

6. You risk your future.
One incident of drug use could make you do something that you will regret for a lifetime.

7. Everyone gets hurt.
Using drugs puts your health, education, family ties and social life at risk.

8. Drugs don't solve problems.
Using drugs won't help you escape your problems, it will only create more.

9. Real friends don't.
If you know someone with a drug problem, be part of the solution. Urge your friend to get help.

10. Drugs don't mix with sports.
Your body and your mind are the keys to your success on the field. Don't do anything to compromise them. You need their total performance every time.

Questions About Marijuana

Why do young people use marijuana? There are many reasons why some children and young teens start using marijuana. Most young people use marijuana because they have friends or brothers and sisters who use marijuana and pressure them to try it. Some young people use it because they see older people in the family using it.

Other users may think it's cool to use marijuana because they hear about it in music and see it used in TV and movies. But no matter how many shirts and caps you see printed with the marijuana leaf, or how many groups sing about it, you should know this fact: You don't have to use it just because you think everybody else is doing it. Most teens (seven out of ten) don't!

More negative effects of marijuana include:

• Problems with memory and learning

• Distorted perception (sights, sounds, time, touch)

• Trouble with thinking and problem-solving

• Loss of coordination

• Anxiety and panic attacks

These risks are even greater when other drugs are mixed with marijuana, and users do not always know what drugs are given to them or even what other drugs are in the marijuana they buy.

One of the biggest hazards of marijuana for teens is this: The drug can make you mess up in school, in sports or clubs, or with your friends. If you're high, you are more likely to make stupid mistakes that could embarrass or even hurt you. If you use it a lot, you could start to lose energy and lose interest in how you look and how you're getting along at school or work. In addition, there is a strong link between drug use and unsafe sex and the spread of HIV, the virus that causes AIDS.

What are the long-term effects of marijuana use? Findings so far show that regular use of marijuana or THC may play a role in some kinds of cancer and in problems with the respiratory, immune and reproductive systems.

- **Cancer:** It's hard to know for sure whether regular marijuana use causes cancer. But it is known that marijuana smoke contains some of the same, and sometimes even more, of the cancer-causing chemicals as tobacco smoke. Studies show that someone who smokes five joints per week may be taking in as many cancer-causing chemicals as someone who smokes a full pack of cigarettes every day.

- **Lungs and airways:** People who smoke marijuana often tend to develop the same kinds of breathing problems that cigarette smokers have. They suffer frequent coughing, phlegm production, and wheezing, and they tend to have more chest colds than non-users.

- **Immune system:** Animal studies have found that THC can damage the cells and tissues that help protect people from disease.

- **Reproductive system:** Heavy use of marijuana can affect both male and female hormones. Young men may experience delayed puberty because of THC effects. Young women may find the drug disturbs their monthly cycle (ovulation and menstrual periods).

Does marijuana lead to the use of other drugs? Long-term studies of high school students and their patterns of drug use show that very few young people use other illegal drugs without first trying marijuana. Using it puts children and teens in contact with people who are users and sellers of other drugs. So using marijuana creates more risk that a user will be exposed to and urged to try more drugs. However, most do not go on to use other illegal drugs.

Public, government and media attention to cocaine and crack in recent years may have led some adults and young people to assume that marijuana is of less concern. Many of today's parents experimented with marijuana earlier in their lives and may be uncomfortable counseling their children against its use. Some of those arguing for legalization promote the idea that marijuana is "no big deal," or that marijuana may even have benefits. But, from my point of view, and I've seen a lot where this is concerned, marijuana is nothing but trouble. It is a quick way to derail your dreams of being a pro someday. Remember the big three-attitude, discipline and commitment. Marijuana violates all three of these rules. It is hard enough becoming a pro. Why on earth would you work against yourself by using marijuana?

Alcohol Use

Alcohol is another way you can quickly work against your dream of becoming a professional. Like marijuana, alcohol does nothing to make you a better player, a better student, or a better person and it works hard to keep you from success in all three areas. Much of what I've told you about marijuana is true of alcohol; some of the diseases may be different, and alcohol may damage other parts of your body, but the result is the same. The result is that you hurt your chances to be a pro when you drink.

Alcoholism is a disease. People who have the disease lose control over their drinking and are not able to stop without help. They also lose control over how they act when they are drunk.

Doctors don't know all the reasons why people become alcoholics. Some start out drinking a little bit and end up hooked on alcohol. A person might drink to forget problems or to calm nerves, then end up needing alcohol to feel normal. Once a person loses control over drinking, he or she needs help to stop drinking. This includes young people. This includes you.

You all know somebody at school with a drinking problem who is not aware he or she is ill. Even when the alcoholic becomes aware that something is wrong, he or she may not believe that alcohol is the problem. This is especially true of young people. An alcoholic might keep blaming things on other people, on their parents, on their school, or their looks, or the fact that they are shy. Really, it's the alcohol that's the problem.

Tragically, about 11 million children in our country are growing up with at least one alcoholic parent. There are a few in your class right now. And remember, some adults grew up with alcoholic parents too. If you know a student with an alcohol problem, here is some advice you might give:

• Talk to someone you trust about the problem. Talk to a teacher, a Scout leader, a coach or a school counselor.

• A group is available for kids who have alcoholic parents called Alateen. Alateen has meetings, like a club, and the kids share tips on how to make life easier. You can look for the phone number of Alateen in the phone book or call directory assistance for the number of Alateen.

• Someone at Al-Anon or the Alcoholics Anonymous answer line can probably tell you how to find the meetings, too. Ask at school if there are any Alateen groups or school-sponsored support groups.

Here are some do's and don'ts:

DO   Talk about how you feel. You can talk with a safe person in your life – maybe a close friend, relative, school counselor, teacher, minister or others. Sharing your feelings is not being mean to your family. When you talk to someone, you might feel less alone. Talking to someone about your feelings can help you feel less alone.

DO   Try to get involved in doing enjoyable things at school or near where you live – the school band, softball, Boy or Girl Scouts. Doing these activities can help you forget about the problems at home and you can learn new things about yourself and about how other people live. Football did this for me.

DO   Feel normal. Being afraid and alone is the way it is when you live with alcoholic parents. It's confusing to hate the disease of alcoholism at the same time you love your alcoholic parent. All people have confusing feelings: two different feelings at the same time. This is the way many kids feel about alcoholic parents.

DO   Remember to have fun! Sometimes children with alcoholic families worry so much that they forget how to be "just a kid." If things are bad at home, you might not have anyone who will help you have fun, but don't let that stop you. Find a way to let yourself have fun.

DON'T   Ride in a car when the driver has been drinking if you can avoid it. It is not safe. Walk or try to get a ride with an adult friend who has not been drinking. If your parents are going out to drink somewhere, try not to go with them. If you must get in a car with a drinking driver, sit in the back seat in the middle. Lock your door. Put on your safety belt. Try to stay calm.

DON'T   Think that because your parent is an alcoholic you will be one, too. Most children of alcoholics do not become alcoholics themselves.

DON'T   Pour out or try to water down your parent's alcohol. The plain fact is that this strategy won't work. You have no control over someone else's drinking. You didn't make the problem start and you can't make it stop. It is up to your parent to get treatment. What your parent does is not your responsibility or your fault.

Tobacco Use

"Let me ask you this: Is there anything more heartbreaking than seeing a child smoking a cigarette or stuffing tobacco into his cheek? A child hooked on a product he's too young to buy legally? A child making a choice now that could cut her life short later?" -Secretary of Health and Human Services, Donna Shalala, 1998.

Tobacco is truly a teenage wasteland. While the number of teens who smoke cigarettes is increasing, the number of teens using smokeless tobacco or "chew" is leveling off. A recent survey in Missouri indicated that only 14 percent of high school seniors are current users of smokeless tobacco; of these, only one-third are daily users.

Many students-athletes will be exposed to smokeless tobacco throughout their high school and college careers. Some athletes believe that smokeless tobacco is less harmful to their athletic performance than smoking tobacco (i.e., cigarettes, cigars, pipes, etc.) *They couldn't be more wrong.* The short-term effects and consequences of using smokeless tobacco include the following:

• Rapid absorption of the stimulant nicotine through the mouth and into the bloodstream.

• Increased heart rate and blood pressure.

• Constricted blood vessels.

• Addiction to nicotine.

• Reduced physical performance and/or productivity.

- Chemicals in the tobacco produce three carcinogens (cancer causing agents), which, when combined with saliva, produce even more carcinogens.

- Smokeless tobacco can lead to development of lesions in the mouth called leukoplakia, which are considered to be precancerous.

- Damage to gum tissue can result from smokeless tobacco.

- Increased sensitivity to cold and heat can result.

- Your teeth, which can be loosened, can eventually fall out.

- You may have reduced sense of taste and ability to smell.

That's a long list of dangers! When so many children are still using spit tobacco today, leveling off is not good enough. More than a million children and teenagers still use spit tobacco. Nearly one out of every ten high school seniors uses spit tobacco. And among the high school seniors who use spit tobacco, 23 percent tried it by sixth grade, 53 percent by eighth grade and 73 percent by ninth grade.

You have to be a "dip" to use spit tobacco. Spit tobacco is not cool. It's gross. It's addictive. It causes cancer and other health problems. It could take you out of the game. It could even kill you.

Familiar faces/familiar places

Every season amateur and professional athletes make decisions that compromise their ability to be successful or even jeopardize the lives of others. Although it is something that we don't like to discuss because of its negative nature, you, as an aspiring professional, must live with the consequences of your actions. You must be alert for distractions that can jeopardize your career and, in some cases, your life. Several incidents involving drugs, alcohol and/or violence by professional athletes have raised the serious question, "Why?" Because professional athletes make a lot of money and are extremely wealthy compared to the average person, why do some make choices that are bad for their careers and, in most cases, their lives?

One of the greatest players ever to play the game of professional football was arrested for purchasing drugs from an undercover police officer. Former New York Giants linebacker Lawrence Taylor, elected to the Pro Football Hall of Fame in 1999, was arrested in a Florida hotel room on Oct. 18, 1998, for the purchase of crack cocaine from an undercover police officer.

And of course there are problems with alcohol - numerous incidents involving alcohol and drunk driving every year. Some of them end in a simple arrest and community service. Others end more tragically.

Also in 1998, St. Louis Rams rookie linebacker Leonard Little was tested at nearly twice the legal limit for alcohol when he was involved in a traffic accident that killed a St. Louis woman. Little was celebrating his 24th birthday at a downtown hotel bar before the accident. Now he has tragically changed the lives of others and will have to live with the incident for the rest of his life.

The abuse of alcohol and drugs has been the subject of several studies ranging from sports psychology and the professional athlete to the study of healthy lifestyles of the American blue-collar worker. These studies try to make sense of society's need to have stimulants and depressants for citizens to be comfortable. Since a professional athlete depends on his or her body to perform, it would make sense for us to take better care of ourselves - and you, too.

Next to alcohol and drug abuse, the possession of firearms by professional athletes has seemingly increased. A former NBA Rookie of the Year was convicted on a weapons charge and a head coach of an NFL team was caught carrying a hand gun in his luggage at an airport.

In 1995, Seattle Seahawks wide receiver Brian Blades accidentally killed his cousin Charles, who was trying to keep Brian from taking the gun to his brother's house and using it to break up an argument. They struggled with the gun and it went off, fatally wounding Charles.

Facts about handguns:

• According to the *Journal of the American Medical Association* (June, 1992), the leading cause of death for both black and white teenage boys in America is gunshot wounds.

• Every day in America, 14 children, ages 19 and under, are killed in gun accidents, suicides and homicides. Many more are wounded. (Source - National Center for Health Statistics, 1998)

Why do players carry guns? An article published by *The New York Times* in 1997 states that players are more likely to carry handguns as a form of protection because of their high profile occupations. Research done for "Outside the Lines," a story produced by ESPN concluded 145 professional athletes and sports figures were arrested in a total of 134 alleged crimes in 1997. In addition, courts adjudicated 15 crimes from previous years. That's 160 total cases in one year. The study concluded a new incident of crime is committed by a professional athlete every two days. That did not include crimes not reported in the media. The study didn't include those athletes now retired from participating in professional athletics or those who have had judgment decreed against them.

Results of the findings:

• Athletes often took their aggression outside the games.

• Half of the incidents were violent in nature.

• The professional athlete often used physical force during the course of the incident.

• Athletes were just as likely to attack women as men.

• Attacks against women were in a form of domestic violence, sexual assaults or rapes.

• 36 incidents that involved drugs or alcohol, most often in cases related to marijuana possession or drunk driving.

• Many allegations were ultimately dismissed. And for those athletes and sports figures whose cases were resolved and did lead to a conviction, few of them went on to serve any jail time.

The fact that athletes live in the public eye gives an opportunistic person a chance to make accusations and perhaps take a shot at a star in the courts. These people will also try to hit the jackpot by manipulating the media to their advantage. For example, if you are in a crowd and a person baits you into a confrontation by stepping on your shoes, don't grab them or respond physically. They may try to create a suit against you for battery in hopes of receiving compensation. Although it may sound ridiculous this very thing has actually happened.

As a student-athlete you may be just as vulnerable to these situations. As a leader, you must use good judgment. You cannot lead once in a while; you have to lead all the time.

On the Happy Side...

It's fun having everyone know who you are and it sometimes is overwhelming to believe you actually made it to the pros. I know because, after being in the NFL for almost ten years, I still get overwhelmed at what I accomplished getting here. I have to pinch myself to make sure that it's real.

Think about the feeling you have now if you're a popular athlete and multiply it tenfold. That's the experience you have as a young professional. One of the most uplifting feelings, as a professional athlete, is the joy and inspiration you bring to the fans.

Part of that inspiration is the attitude, discipline and commitment you demonstrate in your sport. What fans see when they watch you perform is the best a human being can do with body and mind, a glimpse of the best of the human soul. You are a leader when you play, like it or not. All the times you've been a leader growing up show through your uniform on game day.

Help numbers

American Council for Drug Education
164 West 74th Street
New York NY 10023
212-758-8060
1-800-488-DRUG

Families Anonymous, Inc.
P.O. Box 3475
Culver City, CA 90231-3475
310-313-5800
1-800-736-9805

Nar-Anon Family Groups
P.O. Box 2562
Palos Verdes Peninsula, CA 90274
310-547-5800

Narcotics Anonymous (NA)
P.O. Box 9999
Van Nuys, CA 91409
818-773-9999

National Council on Alcoholism and Drug Dependence
12 West 21st Street, 7th Floor
New York, NY 10010
1-800-622-2255

National Clearinghouse for Alcohol and Drug Information
P.O. Box 2345
Rockville, MD 20847-2345
301-468-2600
1-800-729-6686

National Families in Action
2296 Henderson Mill Road, Suite 300
Atlanta, GA 30345
404-934-6364

Center for Substance Abuse Treatment
Information and Treatment Referral Hotline
11426-28 Rockville Pike, Suite 410
Rockville, MD 20852
1-800-622-HELP

Chapter 9
Managing time, managing you

Time management

Spare time is scarce during any athletic season on any level. How you manage time can play a big role in your happiness and success. The excitement surrounding a season is sometimes deflated by the time commitment required every day in preparation and practice.

A typical day in professional football begins at 6:30 a.m. with weights followed by meetings at 8 a.m. By the time you hit the field, it's 1 p.m., then you don't get off until 4 p.m. By the time you leave for the day, it's close to 5:30 p.m. That's not far from the schedule you have today, with school mixed in. Of course, you have homework to be done at night and, in the pros, homework may involve the study of a playbook or popping a video in the home VCR to study an opponent.

How can a person go through a typical workday and be productive if they've been out all night? The answer is you can't be. You can't because you're too tired and your mind isn't sharp. You make mental mistakes, you're just a bit too slow, in the end you can't help the team be successful. What you do in your personal time will determine how you perform in the classroom and on the field.

There is a time and a place for you to party. If you have the same goals and expectations as the organization you work for, or your coach and teammates in high school or college, your lifestyle and your approach to your job will show it.

Check yourself
Time management is about making effective use of your time. Creating favorable situations so that you can have maximum success.

What is Your Blueprint?

It became just as easy for me to study on breaks during the school day and after school as it was for me to stay after practice longer to perfect my technique throwing the discus. See, I was using the same blueprint to improve myself as a student as I was to improve my abilities as a discus thrower. My plan was to use time available to its fullest, and, ultimately, to outwork the other guy.

My high school schedule was tightly structured because I had to travel a considerable distance. Though it created a long day, the discipline I learned from getting up early and conducting my daily routine was a great preparation for college responsibilities. You might find out the same thing. Because of classes, practice schedules and games, you may not realize how much you're laying the groundwork for discipline in time management for college.

So, You Want to be a Pro?

It took discipline to get up each weekday at 5 a.m. to catch a 5:45 bus. The real adventure was trying to get done with practice in time to catch the last bus home after school. Football, wrestling, basketball, track, handball and weightlifting all seemed to finish after my regular bus made its last pickup. When I missed that bus, I had the opportunity to walk to the nearest bus stop and wait, for whatever bus was coming next. Sometime I wouldn't get home until 10 or 11 p.m. I did this for my entire high school career. Was it easy? No. Was it worth it? Absolutely.

A college football scholarship was something I wanted and wanted badly, so I committed myself. I sacrificed, maintained discipline and kept a positive attitude because I was confident the circumstances would eventually fall in my favor if I kept on working hard.

College for the student-athlete can also be a lot of fun if (and that's a big "if") you manage your time wisely. The excitement of meeting coeds, breaking away from home and being on your own is a rush. The only person responsible for you is you. The university environment will challenge your ability to focus on priorities and obligations. No one is there to wake you up in the morning to get your breakfast for you. No one is there to tell you it's time to do your homework or go to bed. You have all the adult responsibilities you have always wanted. So what's the big deal?

Being in a new environment that is exciting and reactive to your personal input can be overwhelming. Believe it or not, sometimes it's hard, even difficult, to get out of bed because it's so easy not to do anything at all. If you fall into this trap, you are likely to fall behind in school, which could lead to expulsion and academic probation which, in turn, leads to athletic probation and/or the loss of your scholarship. How do you prevent this? Find a routine that keeps you focused on school and allows you to still have a good time. College is supposed to be fun. Don't make it a nightmare.

It is important to find a routine that fits your needs. If you put together a morning schedule that gets you going and coordinate the rest of your day around school, you could make the most of your time. Align your schedule around common activities like bedtime, breakfast, studying and practicing your sport. This way, you maximize your time and create a productive environment for yourself. A routine I discovered that still works for me is the following:

1. Prepare the night before

This will save you valuable time trying to figure out on the run what's next. Have a planner so you can write what your day will be like. Lay out all your necessary clothes and place items such as books and keys, in a visible place so you won't forget them.

2. Set your bedtime

This will give you a deadline to complete your social life and allow you to get proper rest. Turning in between 9-10 p.m. is good; it allows you to get at least eight hours sleep. This helps me because I am an early riser, which means I don't have to rush out the door.

3. Rise early

The worst thing you can do on a college campus is try to sleep until it's time for class. It's always best if you get up and get your day started so that you are alert and attentive in class.

4. Shower/Get dressed

Since you will probably live in a dormitory as a freshman, save yourself some time in the morning. Get dressed before going down to the dining hall and bring your backpack along for class. No need running back and forth.

5. Breakfast

There is nothing like a good breakfast to get your day started. The experts have always said that breakfast is the most important meal of the day, and it is. A good breakfast will help you get the juices flowing and the blood flowing to your brain in the morning to get your day started.

6. Be early to class

Having an efficient routine in the morning will allow you extra time to get to class. Imagine that: A window of opportunity to review your notes or talk to a classmate about something pertaining to class. This is an opportunity to talk to your professor and run a couple of ideas by other people.

Putting together a schedule that allows you to be on time and productive is essential for a student-athlete. Organizing your day around classes, study time and obligations to your sport will enable you to maintain focus. Now that we've discussed ways to get our morning started, let's organize our day.

As a student-athlete, it is important to remember you are a student first. This means your daily class schedule is built around the minimum number of hours every student has to enroll in to be considered a full-time student. In addition, every department and major has a set of courses that every student must complete. This was my daily schedule with four classes during football season.

Daily Schedule

Monday Wednesday Friday

Time	Event
6:00	Alarm off
6:30 - 7:00	Breakfast
7:30 - 8:20	Class
8:30 - 9:10	Read and/or finish assignments
9:20 - 10:10	Class
10:20 - 11:10	Lunch (Study)
11:30 - 12:20	Class
12:05 - 1:20	Dormitory or stadium
1:30 - 5:30	Practice
6:00 - 7:00	Dinner
7:00 - 9:00	Study
9:00 - 10:00	Free Time
10:30	In bed (sleeping)

Tuesday & Thursday

Time	Event
6:00	Alarm off
6:30 - 7:00	Breakfast
7:30 - 8:30	Study (read and/or finish assignments)
9:00 - 10:20	Class
10:30 -12:30	Lunch (Study)
12:45 -1:20	Dormitory or stadium
1:30 - 5:30	Practice
6:00 - 6:30	Dinner
7:00 - 8:20	Class
9:00 - 10:00	Review
10:30	In bed (sleeping)

Saturday is Game Day (if football)

Sunday

Time	Event
7:00	Breakfast
7:30 - 2:00	Free Time
2:30 - 5:00	Study
5:00 - 6:00	Break
6:00 - 7:00	Dinner
7:00 - 9:00	Study
9:00 - 10:00	Free Time
10:30	In bed (sleeping)

Check yourself

Sometimes managing the people around you is the hardest thing about time management.

If you want a blueprint for making it to the pros, try my schedule. It worked for me. If you want a blueprint for going home after your freshman year of college and never being heard from again, try living the party life at night and sleeping until noon.

My schedule isn't the only one that works. Obviously, the schedule structure changes for different sports and that's where you need to work out the best schedule to suit your respective sport. My kind of schedule may be totally out of whack for the kind of schedule you need if your sport involves games or matches in the middle of the week.

Beyond college, my schedule structure could be attributed to the routines I started in high school. After the tryout camp for the World League at Sacramento State, I was invited to the combine in Orlando, but still held my position with Procter & Gamble. Through time management, I carried on my duties with P&G while maintaining a workout pace that allowed me to be in the best shape I could.

I worked out for the two months prior to the combine and I was ready. I handed in my resignation to Procter & Gamble two weeks prior to the day I was supposed to leave for Orlando. They didn't ask any questions; they just said, "Thank you and good luck." The two weeks passed quickly; the next thing I remember I was on a plane headed to Florida carrying a workout bag with a pair of those red baseball shoes, sweats, t-shirts, shorts, a pocket full of prayers and a head full of dreams.

In between my first two Chiefs training camps, my time management went crazy because I went through that ultimate tease from the first training camp and held onto the hope of making it in pro football, unaware of the forthcoming letter from the Chiefs.

I worked as bouncer at a nightclub in Portland on Wednesday, Friday and Saturday nights from 9 p.m. to 3 a.m. To stay in shape, I had two options. Get up and go to the gym at 4:00 in the morning when the crowd was smaller or go after work at 6:30 p.m. when it was crowded. I actually had to do both. When I worked nights, I went to the gym after my day job for two hours, then went home and changed. If it were a Monday or a Tuesday, I worked out at 4 a.m. so that I could go to bed early and catch up on my sleep. To save money, I ate 10-cent bags of noodles and became a vegetarian.

That was my routine for four months until the Chiefs sent me that letter inviting me back to another training camp. That's called commitment. Nothing less will do.

Understanding and using time management skills is essential to your success as a student-athlete. These, along with personal management skills, can help you focus and manage situations in your personal life. Personal management and life skills teach you how to handle everyday situations that can create unwanted pressures and bad decision-making. Learning life skills can give you a sense of confidence and empower you to take on any challenge. Life skills teach you how to avoid situations that can distract you, cause indecisiveness and destroy all that you have worked to accomplish.

Give me a little time

Let's talk about *your* time. And how efficiently you use it. You know, there is an old saying which goes something like, "If you have a project that needs to get done, give it to someone who is busy."

For a young person, that may seem like a heavy concept. If so, think about it for a moment. It may sound obviously ridiculous, but when you're most productive, you're getting the most done. And when your workload is increased, you can effectively handle the increase because you've established good work habits.

Let's back up for a moment. Let's say you are just kind of hanging out, laid-back, and really not getting much done. You have homework to do - but you don't feel like doing it. This is a low mode of productivity.

If you had a project which needed to get done in a quick and orderly fashion, obviously the person in high mode of getting the work out would get the nod.

It does sound all too simple. It is, nonetheless, true. I've seen it over and over again.

It is also true that having a lot of physical and mental energy in our daily lives is not a constant. Some days are better than others. There might be high productivity on Monday and Laid-Back City on Wednesday. That is the way many of us live.

Because that is true, we all need to bring a time-discipline of some kind to our lives if we are to be successful. In that spirit, I challenge you to implement a schedule similar to the one I outlined earlier in this chapter.

You can use the exact one, I don't care. Do it for a week - don't quit. And evaluate your results on Sunday. See how you liked it and - the plusses and minuses. Then fine tune it to fit your schedule better, if necessary.

Some people say it takes ninety days to form a habit. So, with a new structure in your life, you are going to have to stay with it for it to become permanent.

Once a familiarity with your schedule is attained, I'll bet you find it at least somewhat beneficial and enjoyable.

One thing I ABSOLUTELY GUARANTEE, though. If you organize your time better for athletics and school work, use it more efficiently, guess what happens? You have more free time to relax, hang out, be with your friends, go to movies and the like.

So start managing your time better - start now! Good luck!

The future is a long time

Use the exercise following to do a survey of yourself and your immediate family. In it, you can begin to put on paper some long-term personal and career goal-setting, similar to academic goal-setting you did in Chapter 7.

Check yourself
Have a purpose for each day.

Exercise

Get To Know You

What is your full name and age?

_____

What do you prefer to be called?

_____

When were you born and where?

_____

What is your mother's name and age?

_____

What is your father's name and age?

_____

What is your brother's name and age?

_____

_____

What is your sister's name and age?

_____

_____

Favorite subject in school

_____

Favorite sport(s)

_____

So, You Want to be a Pro?

Favorite hobbies

_____

What are some things that you do to help out at home?

_____

What are some of the things that you are most proud of?

_____

What is your favorite food(s)?

_____

When was the last time you rewarded yourself for getting good grades?

_____

Write four things that you like most about yourself

_____

_____

_____

_____

Write four things that you love about yourself

_____

_____

_____

_____

Do you plan to attend college?

_____

How far do you plan to go in college? (i.e., MBA, Ph.D.)

_____

Where do you plan to be in 5 years?

_____

_____

_____

Where do you plan to be in 10 years?

_____

_____

_____

What are some goals that you would like to accomplish by age 20?

_____

_____

What are some goals that you would like to accomplish by age 30?

_____

_____

What are some goals that you would like to accomplish by age 50?

_____

_____

If you were to live to the age of 100, what would you like to be remembered as or how would you like to be remembered?

_____

_____

Chapter 10
Other success stories

Today, more than any other time in the history of professional athletics, there is a positive push for girls to become professional athletes. Women like golfer Nancy Lopez, trackstar Jackie Joyner-Kersee, tennis player Martina Hingis, Lisa Leslie, WNBA star Rebecca Lobo and many others, are helping change the way we look at women in professional sports. Sports are an integral part of our society. Girls can participate in sports with their peers just as well as boys, yet they are sometimes discouraged. The entire world is starting to recognize the importance of opening opportunities for girls, so they have the chance to dream like boys. Women who have had the opportunities to compete as professionals have succeeded financially, professionally and emotionally.

One of the premier players in the Women's National Basketball Association (WNBA), Lisa Leslie, says she had no paternal support. She has met her father only once since he left her family. And she was only four at the time. Lisa's mother, Christine Leslie, was a truck driver. Once Lisa started playing basketball, her mother was hardly around to watch because she was supporting Lisa and her two sisters. Lisa continued to develop her talent despite the emotional obstacles of her family life, and scored 101 points for Morningside High School, Inglewood, Calif., before the opposing coach refused to continue after halftime. Another great female athlete, Cheryl Miller, holds the national single-game record with 105 points in a high school game.

Miller was a four-time All-American at USC where Leslie's path also led for her college education.

Other female athletes like figure skater Kristi Yamaguchi and gymnast Nadia Comaneci are great examples of the possibilities available to women who decide to get involved in sports as a way to improve their lives. Yamaguchi catapulted from her success in the Winter Olympics to a lucrative professional skating career with numerous endorsements. Though Comaneci and other gymnasts have few options professionally, Comaneci today spreads her knowledge of the sport to young, aspiring athletes in a gym she co-owns with her husband, former Olympics gymnastics gold medalist Bart Connor, in Norman, Oklahoma.

Donna Shalala, secretary of Health and Human Services, cited a report that says girls who compete in sports or work at physical fitness can feel better about themselves and improve their chances at success in life. According to the President's Council on Physical Fitness and Sports, female high school athletes tend to get better grades and are less likely to drop out than non-athletic students. They also are more likely to go on to college and develop fewer chronic health problems. Research shows that girls who participate in physical activities usually are more mentally fit and develop social skills more easily than those who are less active.

High school girls (and boys) who participate in sports have higher grades than non-athletes. In addition, a larger percentage of athletes scored in the top quartile on a standardized test. Furthermore, high school athletes are more likely than non-athletes to aspire to be leaders in their communities as adults. If girls are to grow up to be leaders, they need comparable opportunities to develop their leadership skills through team sports.

Participating in sports has also been found to increase young women's (and young men's) self-esteem. High school athletes are more likely to describe themselves as "highly popular" than non-athletes.

Unfortunately, even girls who participate in sports and fitness cite obstacles, such as boys who refuse to pass balls to girls, or who criticize girls' performances; girls getting picked for teams after all the boys are picked; gym teachers who assume girls are not as good as boys; and better coaches and equipment for boys' teams.

Traditionally, sports have been the training ground for boys to learn about team work, goal setting, the importance of practice and other life skills that contribute to the overall success of the individual. They developed skills for handling pressure situations, living healthy lifestyles, and the importance of sportsmanship and character. This option is opening more and more to girls.

A woman participating in professional athletics is not a new phenomenon. Sports coverage in newspapers, radio and television has focused on the male athlete, but it is evident women have a growing interest in athletics and women's competitive sports. Women's sports programs, foundations and organizations are dedicated to increasing opportunities, providing information and showing the benefits for girls and women in sports.

Jackie Joyner-Kersee,
A Pro For All Seasons

Long after a triumphant return to the track near her hometown of East St. Louis, Ill., Jackie Joyner-Kersee, on the night July 25, 1998, prepared to meet with the media. Several hundred of her fans, chanted, "Jackie! Jackie!" "The U.S. Open: Track and Field Farewell to JJK" track meet had been over a long time but the fans did not want to go home.

They still wanted a piece of JJK. An autograph was in most demand, but a smile would do. She tried to oblige all requests, but every ounce of energy was used up.

Arguably the greatest female athlete ever, Joyner-Kersee found out she was human that night. Only three days earlier, at the Goodwill Games in New York, JJK won the heptathlon gold medal at age 36. It was one of the most courageous performances of her career. Already in her possession were gold medals in the heptathlon from the Olympics in 1988 and 1992, an Olympic long jump gold medal from '88, an Olympic silver medal from '84, an Olympic long jump bronze medal from '92 and '96 and numerous other medals from national and world titles, yet JJK persevered in competing against athletes of the highest level.

The turnaround from the Goodwill Games to the Saturday night heptathlon at the Southern Illinois University-Edwardsville meet, however, was too much. With the fuel tank almost empty, no miracle finishes could vault JJK over the top. But it didn't matter.

"All I wanted to do was to come out and give the home fans

something to remember me by," JJK said after the meet attended by 9,100.

Because of the work performed in her community, coupled with her athletic accomplishments, she couldn't lose. It's been well-documented around St. Louis what JJK overcame to become a great athlete and what she continues to share, not only directly to East St. Louis, but to the entire bi-state metropolitan area.

JJK crystallized her celebrity status, even in the twilight of her athletic career, on that humid July night when she was asked what was next for her.

"Everything I've been doing in athletics," she said, "I always try to parlay that into something else. Something that would be coming back to the community. Trying to build a youth center. Trying to run a sports marketing company. Also, to continue my promotional work and personal appearances. Doing a lot of work for athletic kids and athletic people. So there's a lot that will keep me busy and whatever else I can to do support the sport of track and field."

Amazingly, JJK balanced her training for the Goodwill Games with being a businesswoman and a spokesperson that often demanded out-of-town trips for two to three-week periods. Tune-up meets were out of the question. That's what made her Goodwill Games victory so special.

So what made her the pro she is?

St. Louis Post-Dispatch columnist Bernie Miklasz summed it up the day after the meet ended in Edwardsville: "She conquered a poor childhood, she conquered a sore hamstring, she conquered severe asthma, she conquered disappointment. She conquered the long jump and the heptathlon and her own doubts. She ruled the world, Jackie Joyner-Kersee did."

She could have whined about the short turnaround time from the day she accepted her medal at the Goodwill Games to her attempt to compete at a high level during her farewell meet, but JJK's character surpassed the level of her performance.

"I came into this sport with no excuses. I'm going to leave this sport without excuses," she said afterward.

As a multi-sport athlete at Lincoln High School in East St. Louis, JJK rose above the poverty in her neighborhood and earned a scholarship to UCLA. Part of her leisure was spent shooting baskets at the Mary E. Brown Community Center in East St. Louis, but upon returning home as a UCLA freshman to bury her mother, who died at the age of 37 of a bacterial infection, she found the center was closed.

That closed center created the deep feeling JJK has had ever since, to give back to her community. (The above article was written by Greg Echlin.)

There are many other stories - I have had the chance to meet and hear about some extraordinary people. People who have had personal challenges and tragedies that systematically molded them into who they are today. People whose circumstances and situations created the right amount of pressure necessary to shape them into the diamonds that we see today.

The challenges of adversity and the pressure of society seemingly don't exist in the eyes of these individuals. Their world has long been influenced in ways only imagined in novels and animated on a movie screen. Stories of personal sacrifice and pain shine light on the reality of this cold world of superstars and super egos.

People like Chris Zorich, Terrell Davis and Jamila Wideman have stories that range from broken hearts to broken dreams. Unimaginable events that will forever leave scars that no one can see, but they will always feel.

Chris Zorich

Former Notre Dame All-American and NFL great Chris Zorich will forever be a hero of mine. The son of a biracial couple, he grew up in a one-parent home. He had a speech impediment. He drew racial taunts from both white and black kids.

Biracial. Speech-impaired. Growing up on Chicago's rugged South Side. Talk about tough. His mother Zora, who was white, played an especially meaningful role in his life. She helped him overcome his speech problem. His welfare was her main concern. In fact, it was her life.

Through times of incredible hardship and sacrifice, Chris and his mother, together, somehow kept going. Chris became a high school football star, and decided on Notre Dame because of its high graduation rate of football players (over 90%).

In Chris' senior year at Notre Dame, he won the Lombardi award as the nation's premier college lineman.

He went on to play for the Chicago Bears in the NFL, and is now attending law school at Notre Dame.

His mother died in 1991, and he honors her memory every day of his life. The Zora Zorich Scholarship assists needy students to attend Notre Dame. And Chris has other foundations to help the truly deserving. He hasn't forgotten his roots.

It's no wonder Chris is a fantastic role model. His mother belongs in the Role Models Hall of Fame. She was always there for him in his early difficult years and when he became a star, was his biggest fan.

Terrell Davis

When it comes to success stories, who can deny that of Terrell Davis. Originally a sixth-round draft choice of the Denver Broncos in 1995, Terrell has written his name in the history books as one of the most explosive backs in NFL history. Super Bowl MVP, rushing for over 4,000 yards in two seasons, and he is still as humble as the first day he showed up in Denver. Who would believe that TD was a sixth-string running back or that he almost wasn't drafted. That he transferred from Long Beach State University to the University of Georgia or that he was arrested for trying to steal rims off of a car while he was in college. Who would believe that a guy who runs so smoothly on the football field, who cuts on a dime and powers over defensive backs like a freight train had problems when he was growing up. Problems that we all can relate to in some way or another, but he overcame them. He rose above what had been dealt him, the circumstances that created the person we know today as TD.

Terrell grew up in a rough neighborhood in San Diego, Calif. A place that will forever remind him how far he's come and that will remind him of what he could have been. Growing up with all of his brothers, five of them, Terrell had plenty of examples of male role models. When his parents separated, he and three of his brothers went to live with his father where they were reared with discipline and love.

His father, like my stepfather, believed in a physical form of discipline. Discipline that hardened you to the feeling of pain, discipline that brought tears to your eyes and made you think twice about making a mistake. Discipline that makes the people around you wonder how you stay so focused on your goals. In his book, *Dreams in Motion*, Terrell talks about the night his father shot at him and three of his brothers when he was young.

"He pulled each of us out of bed, lined us up against the wall, pulled out his .38 Special with black electrical tape around the grip, and just started shooting. Right in our direction."

He wasn't trying to hit them, he was trying to toughen them up because he loved his boys, and he wanted them to fear nothing. Well, his tactics may have worked. But no father should **ever** choose such a method to toughen up his sons. He and his brothers learned a lot from their father, and even more from each other. His father died in 1987 due to complications of lupus.

I respect Terrell Davis for who he is and what he has been through. The way he carries himself and for the passion he brings to the game. He has endured a lot to be where he is today and all I can do is wish him continued success.

Jamila Wideman

Like Chris and Terrell, the WNBAs' Jamila Wideman also has a story to tell. One that has changed her life forever. A rising star with the Los Angeles Sparks, Jamila has been widely recognized because of her tenacity and her leadership on the basketball court. The former All-American point guard from Stanford helped lead the Cardinals to three consecutive Final Four appearances before being drafted by the Sparks at the end of the 1997 season. PAC-10 All-Academic first team, there is more to her than just basketball.

Jamila, like Chris Zorich, was a child of an interracial marriage. Disregard the fact that her mother is a lawyer and her father an award-winning author or that she is loved immensely by her brothers and extended family. Disregard the fact that she had a college degree from one of the most prestigious colleges in the land and plans to become a lawyer when she is done playing professional basketball. No, disregard all those things that she has done and regard that which has driven her to run as fast as she can away from who she is. Away from what changed her long ago when she was a child and the world around her was still a mean place.

So, You Want to be a Pro?

Growing up in Laramie, Wyoming, then later in Amherst, Massachusetts, Jamila was forced to internalize pain of not belonging by becoming an exceptional athlete. Being the child of interracial parents created its own problems, but a tragic event would change her forever. In 1986, when I was a freshman in college trying to decide what classes I wanted to take, Jamila was just 10 years old and her brother Jake, the middle child, was 16. No one knows why, but Jake killed another boy in a Flagstaff, Arizona, motel room they were sharing. The result of which effected everyone close, the victim's family, and Jamila in particular. The fact that the entire country knew of her brother's crime, lawsuits were pending and people in the media began meddling into the Widemans' past was all taken in by Jamila.

The reality of her nightmares was as tangible as the ball she learned how to dribble so well. She locked them away in her 10-year-old heart and ran to keep them hidden for years. With every dribble and every game she calmed the storm that changed her from a little girl into a focused adult with the world of responsibility on her shoulders. Basketball became her world where the nightmares ceased.

Not until the possibility that the game may be taken from her does she realize that she has internalized all the pain, of Jake, of being black.

Yes, forget about the little girl that will someday defend the common man because no one else will.

Chris, Terrell and Jamila all continued to keep their eyes on the prize and continue to be the examples we all need. They show us that we are not alone in our experiences and that time can heal old wounds. Their belief in their abilities regardless of the situation made them work harder than anyone around them to reach what they set out to accomplish. Although very tragic in their circumstances, you know that they made it. And they continue to make it everyday.

Chapter 11
You can do anything

Competing with integrity

The level of competition in contemporary sports has reached an all-time high. What's the motivation? To be number one, to win, to get the glory, to get the money. Either way, we have become obsessed with the all-or-nothing approach to athletics and this, without a doubt, has hurt many athletes mentally and physically. We have forgotten what it takes to win and the basic fundamental principles of competition: hard work, preparation and integrity.

Because of this obsession with winning and the rejection of losing, individuals sacrifice their lives for a chance to stand in the winner's circle. People who use illegal drugs and doping agents to enhance their performance have an unfair advantage over their opponents. However, they will feel the effects of their choice long after the thrill of competition has gone.

The recreational use of street drugs, such as marijuana and cocaine, along with the use of alcohol by athletes, not only endangers their lives, but also the lives of others around them. As an aspiring athlete, it is important you understand that winning is not everything. Your life is worth more than gold, silver or bronze, or some ribbon.

Fair competition without the use of drugs, through hard work, preparation, and integrity, can accomplish so much more. *You win as an individual.*

My moment to win as an individual came when I prepared for the combine that led to my first professional football contract. I wanted to be fast and quick in Orlando, which was held before the inaugural spring season of the World League. I wanted to make a statement, me and the red baseball shoes I bought before the workout in Sacramento.

A bus was waiting for every able-bodied twenty-something coming out of the airport. I was one of them. We got into the hotel and went through an orientation on how the day would go, then it was time for bed. For those who could sleep. Morning came quickly. So did the butterflies. We ate breakfast, we boarded the bus, we arrived at the stadium, we were on the field. Like clockwork, we were in and out of each drill. I had my red baseball shoes working. Around cones, over bags, through drill after drill. All they could see was a blur. I'm sure of that. Not only was I competing with who knows how many other guys, I was competing with myself.

All of those teams were looking for players to fill their rosters and I was looking for a team to play on. I ran through bags. I shuffled through shuttles and circled cones. I was competing with at least 100 other guys for my job.

After the last drill, that was it. Everyone could go home now or wait until morning when the flights left. I had given it everything I had. Everything. I was leaving the next day to return to Portland unemployed and looking for a job because I gave up my job with

Procter & Gamble. I was so confident I would make it I didn't worry about what would happen after February. I knew I was going to be in a different city anyway. I went down to Orlando and had a great combine. I was able to run and work out for all ten teams in the league.

I competed with honor, integrity and pride. Now, it was up to the coaches and scouts to believe that Pellom McDaniels III could play football. I flew back home to Portland the next day waiting for the deciding phone call that would validate the confidence I had in my performance. At the end of the week that call came. I was drafted in the fifth round by the Birmingham Fire. I was so excited and so happy that I got down on my knees and thanked God right then and there. Through Him, I had the strength to take the chance and through Him, I had the confidence in my abilities to take the chance.

Am I good enough?

Are you confident in your abilities? Do you find yourself doubting your success? Are you afraid of the unknown possibilities in your future? Do you wallow in self-pity at times because someone said you're fat? Or too slow? Or too short? Do you sometimes question if you are good enough to compete with other students and other student-athletes? These are very real questions you will answer sooner or later. The physiological approach to your success as a student-athlete will be much more difficult than any physical exam or test you will ever take. Having confidence in your abilities, confronting your fears socially, academically or athletically is something you must conquer. How do we change the way we feel? What does it take to achieve a winning state of mind?

The human mind is very powerful. We can almost will our bodies to perform phenomenal feats of strength and endurance. We can withstand an enormous amount of pressure and pain to save the life of a total stranger. Why? Because we WANT to. We have an instinct for survival that makes us focus on set goals or objectives when we are under stress. How do you tap into this state of mind and become a mental giant playing a game?

Like your body, your mind has to be trained for success. You have to create a winning state of mind by creating an environment for yourself that will allow you to be successful.

Believe me, there were times I wondered if I was good enough. Deep inside, I felt I was, but I was hoping somebody else would feel the same way. No time was that more evident than when I tried out for the World League at Sacramento State.

After the tryout in Sacramento, all I could think about on the drive back to Portland was whether I got a fair chance to show I could play. I went back to work the following Monday with Procter & Gamble. I continued to work hard, as I always had. I knew I had a job and it was a good job. I wanted more, but I had to wait for my opportunity. On December 7, 1990, I received a letter in the mail. It was from the World League office in Irving, Texas. I was too nervous to open it. But if I didn't, how could I find out what I wanted to know. Was I good enough?

So, You Want to be a Pro?

I opened the letter and it read as follows:

Dear athlete:

In our recent player review camp in Sacramento, you were given a preliminary physical examination. These examinations were given to players that the World League staff felt had the ability to perform at a higher level. On that basis, I congratulate you.

Because of the time frame and the international nature of the World League, it will be necessary to have a valid passport to be a member of the World League.

This letter is NOT telling you that you will be invited to attend the Orlando Draft Combine in early February, but I would not want your exclusion to be for a lack of a passport. Therefore, I encourage you to get a passport in the event an opportunity occurs for you in the World League.

Thank you for your interest in the World League.

Sincerely,

Chet Franklin
Pro Player Scouting Coordinator

I had a response to my question. Someone thought I was good enough and was willing to give me a shot. Now I had an objective in sight. A short-term goal to get me to my ultimate goal. First, prepare for the combine in Orlando. I had to schedule my workouts around my job to be sure I wasn't hurting either one. Second, I had to make a full commitment to achieving this endeavor, which meant sooner or later I had to quit my job. It was the only way I would be fully committed to putting everything into my preparation. "I'm going to make it," I would tell myself each day. Most importantly, I believed it.

Eventually, I received another letter officially inviting me to the combine, which I eagerly accepted. By my belief I was good enough, I was prepared, and I capitalized on the chance by landing my first job as a professional football player with Birmingham in the World League.

In Birmingham, again I was faced with that question, "Am I good enough?" In Birmingham, I felt the way that hypothetical fan in Humphrey Coliseum felt looking up at the 10,000 to one odds against me.

Throughout training camp in Birmingham I was competing against eight guys for only four positions. Talk about tough odds. To make the situation more interesting, one of the guys competing had been with the Los Angeles Raiders the previous NFL season. Three other guys had played in the Southeastern Conference and all the coaches were from the SEC, so they knew what each player was capable of doing. For all I knew, I was the odd man out.

Not one of the coaches had ever seen me play. I had my work cut out to show them I was a player and I was good enough to make the team. I worked as hard as I could by being the first one at every drill and running full speed in every practice. I concentrated on my job first. I watched extra film and went straight home to bed.

"All my dedication and preparation is going to pay off. Just be patient," I said to myself, then I worked harder.

And then it happened sooner than I thought. One of the linemen got hurt. The player who previously had been with the Raiders blew out his knee in a scrimmage and I was thrust in front of him right before the season began. I was still in a rotation, but that was my big chance. I had a great preseason and made the team. I was one of only four defensive linemen to make it.

Check yourself
Choosing success is all up to you. You are responsible for your happiness.

If you have ever questioned whether or not you were good enough, utilize my six-step guide to success:

1. Create a winning environment
Surround yourself with positive influences, people with similar goals and aspirations. Surround yourself with people who want to get something from life and all its rewards. Avoid negative environments where people are quick to criticize and slow to reward.

2. Set goals
Decide what you want to achieve. I knew I wanted to be a professional football player so I had to map it out step-by-step to achieve this goal. How long would I give myself to make it? What specific details would I need to achieve to be successful?

3. Research

Find out every detail of what it is you want to accomplish. If you want to play professional basketball, you should know *everything* about the game. How much does a basketball weigh? When and where did the game begin? Who is credited with its invention? What are some of the court dimensions? These are some examples of questions you should ask to become an expert. Research is important so you can create a visual picture of the environment in which you desire to succeed.

I had forgotten this important component when I tried to break into the NFL in 1991. After the first World League season, Coach Chan Gailey told me New Orleans and Philadelphia were interested in me when NFL camps opened. I was so excited when he told me I don't think my feet touched the ground as I left the building. As I drove back to my apartment to pack my things, all I could think about was having the chance to play with people like Packers great Reggie White and Vikings star Randall Cunningham. I didn't even think twice about New Orleans as an opportunity. I just went with my gut feeling instead of researching the situation with the Saints.

I drove back to Portland and waited for the summer to end, antic-ipating my flight to the Philadelphia Eagles and the NFL. When I left for training camp at the end of July, 1991, I didn't know what to expect. All I knew was I was going to be on the same team with Reggie White and that was enough for me. To this day I am still awed by the man.

What I failed to do was look beyond the feeling I had for White and, in a practical way, examine if my chances of making the Eagles were better than making the Saints. Because I failed to properly research the situations, as you know, I ended up asking for my release because it didn't work out with Philly. I might have been better off with the Saints.

4. Take pride in your work

Having a strict work ethic and morals will allow you to shine through in times of pressure and stress. Taking pride in your work ethic builds great character. I know my character was tested when I was working for Procter & Gamble because I was still burned up about being undrafted by the NFL.

The job with P&G wasn't difficult at all. I had to sell store managers on the fact that they had products in their corporate warehouse which had to be moved and made available because of an ad coming up in the newspaper. Simple. In addition, my job also included making sure all of our products maintained their proper market share on the store shelves while, at the same time, the shelves were all clean and orderly. I was responsible for more than 130 stores in the Pacific Northwest.

I was dying inside, though. I couldn't stand it. Watching football games on television and seeing guys I played against in college and in high school running around on television playing in the NFL, was hard to take when I was out selling shampoo, deodorant and toothpaste. It wasn't fair, I thought. I worked hard and I was dedicated to preparing and winning. Why didn't anyone pick me in that '90 draft?

That's what crossed my mind every time I sat down to watch a game. I knew I could play; I could compete with any of them.

The events that led to my trip to Sacramento for the World League tryout occurred in a weekend meeting with my boss, the district supervisor. We were taking a break and I happened to walk into the lobby of the hotel we were in when I stopped to watch a game. I think it was the Chicago Bears against the Green Bay Packers and I knew one of the guys playing. After I pointed out the player I knew and talked about how far we went back, he turned to me and asked if I still thought about playing football. I explained how long it had been a dream of mine to have the chance to run out on a field in front of crazed fans.

He said, "Well, Pellom, don't you think that if you were good enough you'd be playing?"

I stopped, looked at him and thought to myself, "What a jerk." But I realized he had a point. If I was good enough, and I thought so, what was I doing there in the hotel? I should have been on television playing against Green Bay, Chicago, Cleveland or Dallas. I shouldn't have been selling shampoo; I should have been selling myself to a team. And, with that, I made the decision to quit my job and pursue my dream.

It was a good job, mind you. I had it made out of college, but I wasn't happy. I didn't have the chance to live my dream and although the message sent to me by the draft oversight was that I wasn't good enough to be included on an NFL roster, I had to be sure of it myself.

Because of my bitterness at being overlooked in the '90 draft, I could have carried a bad attitude to my new job with P&G. On the contrary, I kept my head up, did the best job I could and left the company in good-standing.

5. Be a leader

Your future is in your hands. Don't let others influence or persuade you negatively. Your goals and ambitions are for your enjoyment and satisfaction.

6. Practice conscious decision-making

The fact that you decided to read this book shows that you have actively made the decision to pursue your dreams. *You* made the choice to be a success.

Check yourself

What do you want?

My grandmother used to say, "A closed mouth doesn't get to eat." Meaning, if you don't ask for what you want, chances are you won't get it.

The art of the possible

You can do anything. When someone says, like the title of this chapter, that in effect, "Your future is limitless," young people roll their eyes. "Yeah, right. Where have I heard that one before?"

I like to talk about the art of the possible. Neither you nor I can literally do "anything." We can't leap tall buildings in a single bound. We are not faster than a locomotive. We aren't (get it?) Superman. (With apologies to Superwoman.)

So what is possible? For you. What do you *want* to do? Where are your capabilities, your strengths? The answer to these questions and others are available from educators and counselors in your school.

Many of your already know the answer to these questions about you. Others need to find out.

Get them, then chart a road map, get others involved like teachers, counselors, career mentors, coaches and of course, your family. You'll need a lot of help along the way. And you should welcome it.

Reaching a worthwhile goal is never easy. The road to success will have bumps, maybe even some trainwrecks. For those who succeed in the end, for those who won't be denied, these obstacles are merely detours along the way to their goals.

When I was first denied a shot at the NFL, I remember thinking it was just a postponement. I was always trying to be positive - to shore up nagging doubts that I had from time to time. (Remember attitude.)

Computer software pioneer H. Ross Perot talks about leaving IBM and starting his own company back in the 1960s. He is fond of saying that when some things didn't work out, he refused to acknowledge to himself that he had failed. So he went to Plan B and kept plugging away. He became tremendously successful - and eventually a billionaire, too.

You should know that in life, almost nothing ever goes exactly as planned. In football games, we may have a game plan out the window by the first quarter. Working on Plan B, C or D early on. That's just the way things go.

The important thing to see is progress. It's just amazing what can happen if you get up every day and keep putting one foot in front of the other, and one day - voila' - you've arrived.

The art of the possible. Set goals. Keep your "eye on the ball." Stay with it. You'll get there.

Check yourself
Put together a game plan for success and the game will be a lot more fun.

What is a Time Line?

A time line is a line that has important dates on it that pertain to your life, when you were born, when you lost your first tooth, when you learned to read, when you discovered your particular sport, when you graduated from high school and plan to graduate from college. The purpose of the time line is to put where it is you want to go and how short your time actually is in perspective. The line is divided into five-year blocks of time. The first thing you do is write under the first vertical line your birthday, then mark how old you are today in close proximity to your age. It should look something like the following:

5	10	15	20

After you have placed the two dates, next you want to set your goals. At what age will you graduate from high school? When will you graduate from college? When will you have your first job? When will you buy a car, house and get a pet? When will you get married, have children and retire from working? How long would you like to live? Write these out so that you can see what you would really like to accomplish with your future.

The possibilities of your life are as infinite as the line they are drawn on.

Check yourself

Have you given yourself a compliment today?
- I can do anything.
- I believe in me.
- Everyday is an opportunity to get better.

Setting short-term and long-term goals

Any goal you set should be realistic and achievable. Don't place things so far out of reach you can't see what you're trying to achieve or the steps necessary to achieve it. The examples below represent ideal problems you may have experienced. Below them are goals laid out to attack those problems:

Example problems

1. My English grade is dropping this semester or quarter.

2. It's hard for me to speak in front of the class.

3. I can't seem to pay attention in class.

4. My free-throw shooting is terrible.

Example goals

1. I will do my English homework first at night and get help every day until I get it right.

2. I will raise my hand at least once each day in two of my six classes. I will make notes about what I want to say before I raise my hand. I will practice speaking at home.

3. I will pay attention to the teacher out of respect to him or her and responsibility to myself. I will get more sleep. I will take notes in class which will help me pay attention.

4. I will stay after practice and shoot 100 free throws.

On the next page, write out some problems you have in school, in your sport, in your life, then write your goals in the spaces provided. After one week, review each goal you wrote in the additional space provided.

Check yourself

Success is like an animal, it feeds off of your sacrifice. The more you sacrifice, the more success you will have.

Week 1   Date_____

My Problems
1. _____

2. _____

3. _____

4. _____

5. _____

My Goals
1. _____

2. _____

3. _____

4. _____

5. _____

One Week Review
A. Did you reach your goals?

1. _____(Yes. No, Explain)

2. _____(Yes. No, Explain)

3. _____(Yes. No, Explain)

4. _____(Yes. No, Explain)

5. _____(Yes. No, Explain)

(If not, was the goal too high? Did unavoidable circumstances get in the way? Were you motivated?)

_____

_____

B. How do you feel about your progress?

_____

_____

_____

_____

Wishes and hopes

Some of my "wishes" (short term)

_____

_____

_____

_____

Some of my "hopes" (long term)

_____

_____

_____

_____

If you could change one thing about the world, what would you change?

_____

_____

_____

_____

Check yourself

When working towards an honorable goal, don't listen to those critics whose bravery seems to come from their mouths and whose battlefield is on the sideline.

Chapter 12

Looking back, looking ahead

Leaving Kansas City

Football has given me so much. It has given me confidence and self-esteem. It has given me the opportunity to see the world from Tokyo, Japan, to Barcelona, Spain. It has given me the chance to be successful and taught me lessons I keep close to me. Football has taught me that attitude, discipline and commitment matter. My approach to life has been molded by the Big Three and fueled by my persistence.

One day when I look back on my days as a professional football player, I will be able to say that I played in one of the greatest eras of professional sports. One that witnessed the dazzling feats of Michael Jordan and hailed Wayne Gretzky as "The Great One." A time that saw Sammy Sosa and Mark McGwire battle against history and John Elway lead "HIS" Broncos to consecutive Super Bowl victories. Yes, there are memories and then there are MEMORIES. And I am leaving some very pleasant ones as I head for Atlanta.

I am leaving my family that was Kansas City. I am leaving the people of the quiet and faithful community who loved the smell of freshly mown grass, especially the grass that grew on the field of Arrowhead Stadium. For seven years, I had the opportunity to gaze into the stands - a sea of red - at the shining faces of the people who had adopted me, the faces of the children who admired me because I wore the uniform that had an NFL insignia on the sleeve. Driving past the tailgaters in the parking lot I could hear them shouting, "Good luck Pellom," or "Give 'em hell, Pellom." I'll miss them because they gave me what I always wanted. The support of family.

I had a chance to grow up in Kansas City and find out who I was, and eventually become who I am. Working and living in the community as a volunteer, as a friend and as a husband, brought me closer to those people who supported me and gave me the chance to thank them for their support. If I had to choose just one memory that I could take with me from my time there, I couldn't. I've sacked John Elway and Steve Young, made big hits on Jerome Bettis and Terrell Davis, made tackles to save touchdowns and even played on the same teams with Joe Montana and Marcus Allen.

All those events, all those great names can't seem to replace the people I have had the chance to encounter. My favorite memories would have to include a lady in the stands who gave a few of us a bag of cookies for luck at every home game. Of Papa Joe, who worked maintenance at the stadium and just loved to talk about life. Of Brenda, Bob, Jim, Eileen and Pete who helped me whenever I needed it. It would be of a couple of trainers, Dave and Bud, and how "ice and steam" was the solution to every problem. Of Redman, Russ, Matt, Jeff and Jeff, and how can I forget Andy, who knew how hard I worked to get where I was and never seemed to change no matter how much changed around them. Of Lamonte Winston, you will see in time. Of Marty Schottenheimer and Carl Peterson who opened the door. Of Mr. Hunt: who knows where professional football would be without you? Thank you. To all those who I have failed to mention for lack of pages. I thank you, too.

My wife and I will forever have a special place in our hearts for Kansas City. Navvab has also been very active in the community, serving most recently for Catholic Community Services in Kansas City, Kansas. She leaves behind a record of service with kids, and some pleasant memories as well. She attended Emory University, so moving back to Atlanta will be a homecoming of sorts for her.

For me, leaving the Kansas City Chiefs is not what I anticipated doing, really, or what I wanted to do. Coming up a few days from draft day, I was an unsigned player. The Atlanta Falcons made me an offer. They told me they needed to hear before the draft started. So, I talked it over with Navvab, and gave them a definite yes, a verbal handshake on the phone. I was going to be a member of a team that was defending NFC champs.

The next day, the Chiefs matched the offer. I said no to them.

Although I was not contractually obligated to Atlanta, I had made an oral commitment to them. I said, "I accept your offer." I had given my word. And my word is my bond. It was a matter of integrity. I was a Falcon. After expecting and hoping to retire as a Chief, well, you gotta do what you gotta do sometimes. Things change. Pulling up our deep roots in Kansas City is not easy. Leaving behind the wonderful young people and kids I worked with via my foundation - well, I'll miss them immeasurably.

At the same time, I'm excited about Atlanta. If the Falcons have the same success as before I arrived, I'll see you in the Super Bowl! Kansas City, you will always be a part of me; the experiences, the opportunities you provided me will go a long way. Now that I am a part of the Atlanta Falcons, guess I had better learn how to do "The Dirty Bird."

Conclusion

I hope you have learned that the path to becoming a professional athlete is not easy. You will have to overcome obstacles as well as more important decisions along the way. Although it can be very satisfying and fulfill your dreams, the length of a professional sports career is extremely short. The importance of an education can never be underestimated. You must always be prepared to make the transition to the real world.

The exercises and principles provided in this book are meant to prepare you for a successful life whether or not you make it as a "pro." Remember, *you* define the word pro within your own individual circumstances. I wish you all the luck in the world and hope that you accomplish whatever it is you set your mind to. Good luck and God bless you.

The author was born in San Jose, Calif. He became a member of the defending NFC champion Atlanta Falcons in April of 1999. Prior to that, he was a versatile defensive lineman for the Kansas City Chiefs.

Pellom is certainly one of the most active contemporary professional athletes when it comes to serving his community. In 1993, he established the Arts for Smarts Foundation, which he uses to both expose disadvantaged children to the arts and encourage expressive development and creative thinking. Pellom's Fish Out of Water writing club produces a publication called *Fish Tales for Kids* which is a compilation of students' writing.

Among his many off-field pursuits, he is an author, artist, feature writer, television host, broadcaster and inventor. In 1998, he was named Kansas City Chiefs Man of the Year. He has been featured on *CBS Sunday Morning* regarding his work with children and was chosen by *Ebony Magazine* as one of their top 30 leaders 30 and under in 1998.

Previously published works include *My Own Harlem* (Addax Publishing Group, Inc.) in which Pellom shares his thoughts about his personal renaissance through poetry. He resides in Lawrenceville, Georgia, with his wife, Navvab. (Photo courtesy Steven Van Warner)

A Special Offer

So, You Want To Be a Pro? sportswear and a newsletter will be available soon.

To be on the *So, You Want To Be a Pro?* mailing list, please send your name and address to:

So, You Want To Be a Pro?
8643 Hauser Drive
Suite 235
Lenexa, KS 66215

7 08850 11078 7

01495